"In My Father's house are many mansions, if it were not so, I would have told you. I go to prepare a place for you. And if I go and prepare a place for you, I will come again and receive you to Myself."
John 14:2 & 3. (Jesus speaking)

Heaven is a prepared place for prepared people.
PEOPLE GET READY!

PEOPLE GET READY!

A Unique Devotional Book based on the music of the Baby Boomer Era

Tim & Gina Fortner

First Printing: People Get Ready
Author: Tim Fortner
© 2019
All rights reserved.

Cover Art and Design: Eleos Press
www.eleospress.com
Interior Formatting: Eleos Press
www.eleospress.com

All Scripture, unless otherwise noted, comes from the New International Version, Zondervan, and King James Version of the Holy Bible.

ISBN-13: 9781712930502

FOREWORD

I love a good book, I love music, and I love the Word of God.

It is not every day that the three can be put together in such a way that they make for a read like no other, but that is exactly what Tim and Gina Fortner have done within the pages you are about to journey through.

Music is one of the most beautiful things of life that brings people together and, for many, creates a memory unlike almost anything else this world offers. Much of the time, the memories music brings back are of the kind that places a smile on your face or instantly takes you back to another place in time, often with someone you cared very deeply about. Music can bring soothing to the soul or memories that are hard to bear.

As much as I love music, I love the Word of God even more, and the principles which God gives us to live by in His Word, the Bible.

In this book my friends, Tim and Gina combine their great love of music with their greater love of Almighty God and His Son Jesus Christ. Inspired by the Holy Spirit I believe Tim and Gina have put together one of the most uniquely different and interesting books I've ever had the joy and privilege of reading. It really was a page turner and hard to put down. Every story involves a fascinating take on a song and the story behind it and, more importantly, its cultural relevance and the biblical takeaways we can learn from each one.

What a fun read as one is reminded about so many great songs from our past and the insights drawn from them as only the Fortners can do. It is an ingenious combination all of us can enjoy reading, reliving and receiving a gift in the process. I love this couple and am in awe of the intellect and creative gifts God has given to Tim and I am inspired by Gina's great faith and her love of her husband. After reading this book I know you will understand exactly what I'm talking about. So relive the music, make a new memory and marvel how Tim and Gina lead us back through music to the Maestro of our soul—the Lord Jesus Christ!

Respectfully,
T. Clark Shaw
Casey Jones Village, Jackson, Tennessee

PREFACE

Our nation is at a watershed moment in history. Another national election awaits us in 2020. We seem to be at the fulcrum point of great leverage which is prying us apart as a nation. We used to pledge we were one nation under God and as such indivisible. That used to be us. But now our communities are divided, our families splitting up and our nation is in upheaval.

The causes of these upheavals are many: race, gender, economics, sexual preference and all are being politicized. Politics are a lagging indicator of who we are, what we have become, and are becoming. Every four years they reveal who we are in the platforms of the political parties.

As Christians and as Americans we serve two kingdoms. We only know how to deal with the one kingdom, our beloved America, based on our faith in the kingdom of God which tells us how we ought to live and love.

What poor ambassadors we have been to not more clearly represent what our Leader, the Lord Jesus Christ taught us. Here in clear language He tells us the two commandments upon which His kingdom is based: "Love the Lord your God with all your heart and with all your soul and with all your mind. This is the first and greatest commandment. And the second is like it: Love your neighbor as yourself. All the law and the Prophets hang on these two commandments." (Matthew 22: 37-40)

This is what this devotional is about—the two greatest commandments which are based on love—the most discussed topic, the most powerful emotion for which we were created. We were made to love and be loved. It is also the answer to our problems. It is what man has been seeking since creation.

Could it be this idea of love—unselfish love—is what will solve mankind's problem? What a revolutionary idea!

"There is one thing stronger than all the armies in the world, and that is an idea whose time has come."
                              -Victor Hugo
                              1802-1885

Remember this truth: ideas have consequences.
                              -Tim and Gina Fortner

INTRODUCTION

This 31-day devotional is based on songs of the Baby Boomer era-late1950s, predominantly '60s and '70s.

Each devotional starts with a song title: Example: Our first devotional will be: "People Get Ready, There's a Train a Coming."

I have selected this popular song from the Impressions as our first devotional as it sets the stage for looking at these songs of our youth and what they now mean to us at our age now. So, whether you are in your 50s, 60s or 70s you realize the impact of aging. The Train which is coming is the end of this life, but the beginning of eternity for our souls which, I believe, exist forever. So, the message is: people get ready for this train which is fast approaching. We now realize, unlike the popular Saturday morning show, "Superman" we are unable to stop this speeding locomotive. In fact, it seems to be getting faster every year, doesn't it?

In looking back at these popular songs, we begin to realize the artists quite often were telling us their life stories. Movies use music to enhance their stories. Music is found in the rhythm of the rain, the songs of the birds, and sounds of the street. Music can bring us to tears or set our feet to dancing. But the popularity of a song in my youth depended on "it had a good beat and it was easy to dance to." (American Bandstand's most common criteria for a song's popularity) A 17-year-old's perception of life is a whole lot different from a 70-year-old's perception.

Each devotional will also feature when the song was popular, when the song reached its highest rating on the Top 40 and interesting stories and insight into the artists, the performers, and writers.

From early doo-wop, rock and roll, rockabilly, country and western, folk music, the British invasion and the disco we find what has always been true: each generation tends to have its own music, hairstyles and dress. But now as we contemplate the lyrics of these songs of our times at our current age, we can construe entirely different meanings as they apply to our lives today.

Everyone has different reading habits. Since this book is based on songs, I would suggest you may want to listen to the songs on whatever venue you use, (I-Tunes, etc.) to familiarize yourself or recall the lyrics. Some may want to read the background of the song and about its writers, composers and performers first. There is a Bible verse associated with each song. For the Bible is a book of stories of real people who experienced the same emotions we do.

Enjoy the memories these songs may recall, but take seriously the message, for I assure you as sure as night follows day, there is 'a train a coming!'—and you better get ready!

DEDICATION

Dedicated to my friend, Bill Way

My friend, Bill Way, was a musician who loved music. He loved to sing, write and listen. We collaborated on several projects over the last 50 years. I had intended for this to be a joint venture, but Bill was gone before we began. All of us who knew him, miss him. He had a way with words.
This one is for you, Bill

To my grandchildren:
Jack Irvine, Virginia Irvine and Sloan Fortner
"Oh, sing to the Lord a new song!
Sing to the Lord all the earth.
Sing to the Lord, bless His name.
Proclaim the good news of His
Salvation from day to day.
Declare His glory among the
nations. His wonders
to all the people."
-Psalm 96-

Sing with all your hearts:
Jack, Virginia and Sloanie!

-Pops and Gin-Gin

To a Very Special Group of People:

The Fortner Sunday school Class

From 2002 until 2019, you inspired and encouraged Gina and me. You prayed for us and with us during illnesses. You fed us when we were hungry. You visited us when we were sick. You were generous in your giving to us and meeting our needs. You are more than Good Samaritans—you are family to us and always will be. I can close my eyes and see your faces, smiling, laughing and yes, sometimes crying. We had such a special time together in this part of our journey. I am keeping my promise to you that I would write this book. These songs are for all of you.

-Tim & Gina

TABLE OF CONTENTS

"PEOPLE GET READY"

"To everything there is a season, and a time for every purpose under the heaven. A time to be born, and a time to die."(Ecclesiastes 3: 1, 2)

Do you know what is the single most productive workday in the year? It is the day before an employee leaves to go on vacation. They are making sure they have cleared their desk and workplace of all things which needed to be done. They have made sure they have taken care of everything so they will not be bothered on their vacation. They have saved for this trip; planned and made reservations for the beach weeks ago and now are ready to leave in the morning for a 7-day vacation. And who doesn't love a family vacation?

Yet many people spend more time planning where they are going to spend the next seven days, or what they will do on the weekend than they do planning where they will spend eternity. Now this song made popular in the 1960s had a very religious overtone. It may be that Curtis Mayfield and the Impressions were thinking of the changing times of the '60s, the Civil Rights Movement, the war in Vietnam, and the changes America was undergoing. They were telling people how to get ready for the changes coming. Offering some heartfelt advice on what one needed to do.

But now at our age, most of us have stood at the graveside of a loved one, a parent, a grandparent, a spouse and wondered and mused about the mystery of death. Is there life after death, and what is it like and can we know the truth about this greatest mystery? Yes, I believe we can. And our prayer is that you will be encouraged to read these devotionals with an open mind and nothing more than a desire to know the truth. As a grieving Eric Clapton mourning his son's death wanted to know what their relationship would be in heaven.

So, just as you begin a Google search for vacation spots – why not begin a search for where you will spend eternity.

Here is the invitation of Jesus: "Come and see."

People Get Ready

This song, like many of the songs of the '60s reflected the social and political issues of the day. It has a strong Gospel flavor which created the Chicago R&B music of the '60s. Other notable musicians who recorded this song included Rod Stewart.

Curtis' grandmother was a preacher, and he was raised in the church.

Curtis started playing the guitar when he was seven years old. He was exposed to the gospel music of his grandmother's Traveling Soul Spiritualists Church. It was there Curtis first sang in public.

In 1990, getting ready for a concert, a light rig fell on him, and he was paralyzed from the neck down. He recorded his last song, "A New World Order" In 1994, lying flat on his back and singing one line at a time, as he had to struggle to get air back into his lungs. After several more health issues Curtis Mayfield died in 1999. His music lives on.

Read the lyrics to People Get Ready and you will see, I believe, Curtis was speaking of the 2nd coming of Jesus or what happens when one dies. Curtis used to say he was "a Jesus-loving jazz man."

Mayfield's music still speaks and tells each of us: "People get ready—there's a train-a-coming."

It was more than a good beat and was easy for dancing, it was a message that resonates today.

"ARE YOU LONESOME TONIGHT?"

"The Lord God said it is not good for the man to be alone. I will make a helper suitable for him."(Genesis 2:18)

A person can be alone and not be lonely. At the same time a person can be in a crowd and be lonesome. Loneliness is an emotion which can create fear, depression and sometimes lead to hopelessness. It is obvious God is a people person for He created us for relationships.

Some of the most painful times can come in a young person's life during their school days. Teenagers can be cruel and social media can be a monster which damages and hurts young people so uncertain of themselves. The Bible tells us the tongue is a very powerful tool and it has the power of life and death. However, "Kind words are like honey, sweet to the soul, and healthy for the body."(Proverbs 16: 24) And kind words do not cost anything, yet can accomplish much.

There was a teacher who created something which came to be known as "The List." Each year at some point after everyone had gotten to know each other, she passed out a list to the class which had everyone's name in the class and a blank space by their name. She then instructed them to write something nice they had observed about this person. She then took the list home and over several nights she composed a separate list for each student compiling all the nice things everyone had said about them, without revealing the name of the person who had said it.

It was later in the 1960s at the height of the Vietnam war, this teacher saw in the paper one of her students had been killed in action. She went to the funeral home and several of his classmates were there. In a frame next to his coffin was his copy of *The List*. Worn by years in his billfold, it was carried with him every day. As she cried as she read it, his parents came up and said she was his favorite teacher and this list had been with him since the day he received it. Several other students came up and said they also still had their list; it was precious to them.

"Like golden apples set in silver is a word spoken at the right time." Proverbs 25: 11

You may not be lonesome tonight but look around for there are a lot of lonely people out there. Or perhaps as you are reading this, someone has come to mind you have not seen or spoken to in a while who could use an encouraging word. My grandmother said, "Rudeness is never acceptable, kindness always is."

Jesus said when you did this to the least of these, you did it unto Him. You've got a friend in Jesus, and He is dying to talk to you. Really. Is your name written on the most important list? The Lamb's Book of Life.

"Are You Lonesome Tonight"[1]

Elvis moved to Memphis when he was 13 years old from Tupelo, Ms.

His first record was produced by Sun Records. He went on to become the number one best-selling solo artist in the history of recorded music. He made a string of musical movies in the 1960s and had a series of successful concerts all over the United States. Prescription drugs created health issues and Elvis Presley died at the young age of 42.

His home in Graceland is still visited by thousands per year with people coming from all over the United States as well as other countries, especially Germany and Japan to pay homage to the "king of rock and roll." He was known for his polite manners. He was remembered for his generosity and was a loyal friend. He loved his mother and father dearly.

In the waning days of his career, Elvis in an interview was asked what the King of Rock and Roll wanted most of all. His answer was painfully honest and revealed an insight into a man who was adored by millions. Elvis said, "All I ever wanted was three things: someone to love, someone to love me back and something to look forward to."

---

[1] # 1 on UK Singles Chart; #1 on Cash Box; and #1 on Billboard all in the same year. Written by Lou Handman & Roy Turley in 1926. Producer: Chet Atkins. Elvis Aaron Presley. "The King of Rock and Roll." Released: 1960, by Elvis Presley.

PEOPLE GET READY

It is what we all want. We were created for relationships. The Lord wants you to know you do not have to be lonesome tonight. "Here I am! I stand at the door and knock and if anyone hears my voice and opens the door I will come in and eat with him and he with me."(Revelation3: 20)

You don't have to be lonesome tonight. Let Him in and He will never leave you or forsake you.

"(THEY LONG TO BE) CLOSE TO YOU"

"O, Jerusalem, Jerusalem, you who kill the prophets and stone those sent to you, how often I *longed to gather your children together,* as a hen gathers her chicks under her wings, but you were not willing." Luke 13: 34 (Jesus speaking)

Did you realize Jesus longs to be close to you? Love is the subject of the Bible. Love is the motivation for God's plan of salvation. It was grace which brought it down to man. We are told God so loved the world He sent His Son to die for our sins. Love has been the subject of poems, songs, novels, plays and movies. Here are three facts about love, which you probably already know instinctively:

1. *Everyone is looking for love.*
2. *Why is this true? Because God is love and God made us in His image. He has woven the need for love into our DNA in our mother's womb. We literally came out of the womb looking for love.*
3. *Just as there is a universal quest for love there is also a universal source of love. It is only the love of God, which can satisfy this longing and meet this need for love. God provides a special kind of love; it is called agape. This is a Greek word for the supreme love, the love described in John 3: 16, which loves unselfishly to the point of sacrifice.*

Here is the problem we face: there is a universal source of this love found only in a personal relationship with God. His supply of love is limitless, unconditional and can satisfy the whole world. This is the love the world needs now. How do we get this love from God's heart to those who are in such desperate need of it?

It is for this reason, we have written this devotional book to tell you of the wonders of His love toward others. Jesus said, "By this will all men know you are my disciples that you love one another." As Christians we are supposed to be the "connectors" to this source of love.

How does a baby come to love his/her parents? They come to love them because their parents first loved them. "We love God because He first loved us. God demonstrated His love for us while we were yet still sinners, Christ died for us."

They, (God the Father, God the Son, and God the Holy Spirit) long to be close to you.

"(They Long to Be) Close to You"[2]

A brother and sister duo who started out with the brother on piano and the sister on drums. Later Karen moved from behind the drums to be the front person backed up by her brother on piano and vocals. Her contralto voice and his ability to re-arrange previously recorded songs to fit their styles made them a success. They had numerous # 1 hits and won 3 Grammys. They sold more than 90 million records in their career from 1970 to 1983.

Their career ended in 1983 with the death of Karen who was only 33 years old. Karen's death was from heart failure brought on by her battle with the condition of anorexia. Her death from this disorder increased public awareness of this condition. One of the Carpenter's popular songs was: "We've Only Just

---

[2] This is one of those songs released by several different artists before the right artist made it a hit. It was first released in 1963 by Richard Chamberlin (TV's popular Dr. Kildaire). Later Dionne Warwick recorded it on her album in 1965. Burt Bacharach released his own version in 1968. But it was Richard and Karen Carpenter who re-arranged it with their signature vocal duos and released it in 1970 to become a number 1 hit. Re-released: 1970. # 1 On Billboard for 4 weeks in the summer of 1970. Song writers: Burt Bacharach and Hal David. Performers: Richard and Karen Carpenter (The Carpenters).

Begun." Ironically, not realizing how close she was to the end.

As we grow older we sometimes long for simpler, quieter times. We cannot hide from the persistent and often profane clamor of the 21st century. We must learn to live in the world as it is. If Jesus can calm the stormy seas and tell the wind to be still. He can do the same today in the turbulent waves of social media and unrest. He says, "Be still and know." Spend time with Him in His Word. He longs to be close to you.

"(I CAN'T GET NO) SATISFACTION!"

"For He (God) satisfies the longing soul, and fills the hungry soul with goodness."(Psalm 107:9)

If you were coming of age in the 1960s you will remember this song. It was the first hit in the USA of the British group, The Rolling Stones. It captured the adolescent angst of trying to be cool and accepted but unable to find satisfaction.

The lyrics spoke of driving around in our cars, which we all did as soon as we got our driver's license at age 16. We would drive aimlessly for hours with our friends listening to the radio. Turning it up to full volume when the latest hit song came on and singing along with it. Gasoline was less than 30 cents per gallon, so it did not matter if our family sedan only got 15 miles to the gallon.

We wanted something that was missing. We wanted to be popular. Boys wanted to be good at sports, and girls wanted to be cheerleaders or majorettes. We all wanted to be accepted, liked and popular. We had no clue as to what life was about, or at least I did not. And I am pretty sure neither did my friends. We were insecure. We had adult urges in teenage bodies, which were a formula for disaster . The drug to which we were addicted was approval. It was approval which soothed our insecurity. We were in a hurry to grow up but had no idea what it meant to be grown up. We were prodigals in the making, believing if we could get away from the rules of our parents and live life on our own, what a wonderful life it would be.

We were at a crossroads. It is a crossroad every young person comes to in their life. It is found at the intersection of the pursuit of pleasure and the pursuit of truth. We had entered at the wide gate of the broad way which seemed right to us and besides, everyone who was cool was going this way. We would tell our parents when wanting to go somewhere or to some party, "everyone else is going there."

Like the prodigal son, I went off to college in 1963 at age 17 and wasted my opportunities and my father's money with prodigal living. When the prodigal in the story Jesus told in Luke 15, had spent all he had, there arose a severe famine in that land and he began to be in want. I found myself in the same condition. The life I was living did not satisfy me. Where had I gone wrong? I made a wrong turn. I had to turn around and go back, which is what repentance is. I discovered when you come to the crossroads: "Stand at the crossroads and look; ask for the ancient paths, and where the good way is, and walk in it and you will find rest for your soul."(Jeremiah 6: 16) Make a u-turn and go back to that narrow way. The way you're headed leads to a dead end, literally. When you do, you will find what you have been looking for: satisfaction which fills your soul with goodness! It is found in a person, the person of Jesus Christ.

"Can't Get No Satisfaction"[3]

The opening guitar riff of "Satisfaction" became one of the most identifiable rock guitar riffs in the history of rock and roll. Richards used a Gibson Maestro Fuzz Box for the distinctive sound and rock music was changed forever.

Gibson manufactured 40,000 of the Fuzz Box which was operated by a foot pedal and immediately sold out. In 2004, Rolling Stone magazine and a panel of judges named "Satisfaction" as the second greatest rock and roll song of all time. It came in second to Bob Dylan's "Like a Rolling Stone."

It seemed to resonate, as music so often does, with the times of the 1960s and the coming of age of the Baby Boomers.

It was first aired on the popular tv show, Shindig. The Stones lip-synced the dub they had just recorded.

---

[3] Released June of 1965. Reached No.1 on Billboard in July and stayed there for 4 weeks. Written by Keith Richards and Mick Jagger. "The Rolling Stones," a British rock group. This band has performed over 2,000 concerts since 1962 and are still performing. They are one of the most popular live bands in history. At the writing of this book , the Rolling Stones are planning another tour, but it has been delayed as Mick Jagger has a heart problem which requires surgery.

PEOPLE GET READY

We live in an affluent society in America. However, psychologists tell us affluence breeds boredom. Always looking for something which does not seem to satisfy us for long. It is like our thirst cannot be quenched. Jesus said, if you knew the gift of God and who He was, you could ask Him, and He would give you living water and you would never thirst again. Satisfied. (John 4)

"HELP!" HELP I NEED SOMEBODY

"I will lift up my eyes to the hills—From whence comes my help. My help comes from the Lord, who made the heaven and the earth."(Psalm 121: 1, 2)

Notice the exclamation point behind the title of the Beatle hit, "Help!" It represents urgency. On September 16, 1977, I was a young, 31-year-old man in need of HELP! It was an urgent, life threatening situation. I was straddling the rail of a 10th floor balcony of a hotel in the early morning hours in Nashville, TN. Not only was I straddling the rail, I was pushing up with my sock clad left foot with all intentions of jumping to my death to the parking lot 10 floors below. At the last moment, before gravity took over, I pushed back into the hotel room and prayed this prayer.

"Lord Jesus if you are real, come into this room and into my heart and save me or else I am going to die!" The prayer of a young man in desperate need of help. I was an alcoholic and had been since I went off to college in 1963 as a 17-year-old. I was married for the second time. I was a father for the second time. And I was going to fail at both. I wanted to stay sober, but to save my life I could not stay sober. I hated myself and what I had become. I had tried and tried but was unable to stay sober in 14 years. This was the prayer of an honest doubter who wanted to know the truth. The Lord answered my prayer and I went down on my knees a sot but came up from them a saint. I called AA for the first time in my life and that morning attended my first AA meeting.

I walked in as the meeting was starting and they were reading the 12 Steps of AA. I remember the moment like it was yesterday. I heard the first step and knew I was in a place where people understood my dilemma. I was in a place which would help me find HELP! Here was what I heard: "We admitted were powerless over alcohol and that our lives had become unmanageable. Came to believe a power greater than ourselves could restore us to sanity. I knew I was in the right place. And I began a journey of understanding of my Higher Power.

Jesus said, "My strength is made perfect in weakness."(2 Corinthians 12: 9) I believe this was the greatest lesson the Apostle Paul ever learned and so it was for me. The power of powerlessness. Do you need help? Then Jesus has an invitation which still stands to this day: "Come unto me all you who labor and are heavy laden, and I will give you rest. Take my yoke upon you and learn from Me, for I am gentle and lowly in heart, and you will find rest for your souls."(Matthew 11: 28,29) I do not know what problem you are straddling as you read this. It may seem there is no solution. But I know where you can find help. Nothing is impossible for the Lord. "My help comes from the Lord, who made the heavens and the earth. "

"Help"[4]

John Lennon said in a Playboy interview in 1980, it was one of the songs of which he was proudest. He said it was a personal cry for help for himself. He felt he was overweight. He said, "I was fat and depressed." The whole Beatles phenomena was overwhelming all of them, especially, the introspective, sometimes insecure Lennon.

Everything they had worked so hard for— practiced and perfected their skills for years had made them more famous than they ever could have imagined. Imagine then the frustration of realizing this was not what you thought it was. It led John Lennon to question what it would take to be happy. He was crying out for HELP!

The Beatles were part of what was called the British Invasion. Elvis had been away in the Army, drafted at the peak of his early career. There had been the doo-wop sound out of the Northeast, the folk music of Dylan and Peter, Paul and Mary, but these four young men struck a chord with American

---

[4] Released: April 1965. Reached: Number 1 in the USA, UK and numerous other countries in late summer, 1965. Written by: John Lennon and Paul McCarthy. Recorded by: The Beatles (John, Paul, Ringo & George). HELP! Was also the promo and theme song for the movie, Help! Released in April of 1965. It was their fourth number one hit of six number one hits in a row.

youth with their first appearance on Ed Sullivan in 1964. I was a freshman in college. We crowded around televisions in our dorms and were immediately impacted by their performance. Boys began their very night to comb their hair like the Beatles who would be THE GROUP for the rest of the '60s.

Are you on a journey? Are you a seeker? Trying like so many before you to find the meaning of life? It is a journey common to all of us, rich, poor, famous, and nobodies. I discovered life without God is meaningless.

In this song, John Lennon sounds like a seeker to me. He writes in his search for help: "Now I have changed my mind and opened up the doors." There are a lot of doors which people open in their search. Some are very dangerous and can lead one astray or to physical or mental harm. Jesus said, "I am the door. All who enter will be saved." Jesus said, "I am the Way, the Truth and the Life. No man comes to the Father except by me."

"WHEN WILL I BE LOVED"

Ever ask yourself that question? Had your heart broken? "What then shall we say to these things? If God is for us, who can be against us? He who did not spare His own Son, but delivered Him up for us all, how shall He not with Him also freely give us all things? "Romans 8:31, 32. Wow! Does that direct answer to your question give you hope? It tells us this great truth: "God demonstrated His love for us that while we were yet sinners, Christ died for us." (Romans 5:8) Guess what? God has been seeking you all your life. Are you wondering when will you be loved? Disappointed with life? God's love provides you with hope which does not disappoint.

Unlike the English language which has only one word for love, the Greek language has three words used to describe love. There is "phileo"– brotherly love. Therefore Philadelphia is called the "City of Brotherly Love." There is "eros"– erotic love, sexual attraction. And there is "agape"—unconditional, sacrificial love, the love expressed in the verses above which describes and defines the love of God, Who is Love. Over and repeatedly the Bible tells us of God's love. And mankind has been writing songs, books, poems, letters and making movies all about love from the beginning of time.

We often speak of falling in love as if we stumbled into it. The Bible presents love not as an emotion, but as a fruit of the Spirit. It seems if you can "fall in" love, you can also "fall out of love."

Listen how the Bible describes this godly type of agape love. This love is described in I Corinthians 13: "Love is patient, love is kind. It does not envy, it does not boast, it is not proud. It is not rude, it is not self-seeking, it is not easily angered. It keeps no record of wrongs. Love does not rejoice in evil but rejoices in truth. It always protects, always trusts, always hopes, always perseveres. Love never fails." Who wouldn't want to find this kind of love?

The question, "When will I be loved?" has sent many a person on the search for true love. Are you searching for love? Meaning? Purpose? Are you wondering when will I be loved? God says "then you shall call upon Me and go pray to Me and I will listen to you, and you will seek Me and find Me, when you search for Me with all your heart."(Jeremiah 29) Then you will find what your heart has been longing for—you will be loved by the One who loves you and gave Himself for you!

I hope this love finds you. As Adrian Rogers said, "This is LOVE WORTH FINDING!"

"When Will I Be Loved?"⁵

The Everly Brothers recorded this 'rockabilly style' hit in the RCA studio in Nashville, Tn. The recording session included Chet Atkins on guitar and Floyd Cramer on piano. The Everly Brothers had a string of hits including: "Bye Bye Love," "Wake Up Little Susie," "All I Have to Do is Dream," "Cathy's Clown," and "Bird Dog."

Their career was interrupted by active service in the US Marine Corps. They toured with Buddy Holly. Phil Everly died in 2014.

Linda Ronstadt was the leading female singer in the 1970s. Since then, she has retired and has been diagnosed with Parkinson's Disease.

As a side note, Carrie Underwood selected, "When Will I Be Loved"to perform as a contestant on American Idol in 2006.

When you read the stories of these stars, many had aspired and worked to develop their talents from childhood with the hope and dream of becoming stars. However, many discovered fame is fleeting and the ability to perform at certain levels does not last. The only thing which lasts are the souls of men and the Word of God.

---

⁵ Released: 1960. Written by: Phil and Don Everly (The Everly Brothers). Recorded by: The Everly Brothers. Reached: No. 8 on US Billboard Hot 100 in the summer of 1960. Re-Released by Linda Ronstadt, 1975. Reached: No. 1 on Billboard Country Singles.

"Love never fails. But where there are prophecies, they will cease; where there are tongues, they will be stilled; where there is knowledge, it will pass away. And now these three remain: faith, hope and love. But the greatest of these is love."(I Corinthians 13)

"THE BOOK OF LOVE" (WONDER WHO WROTE THE BOOK OF LOVE)

"All Scripture is given by inspiration of God, and is profitable for doctrine, for reproof, for correction, for instruction in righteousness, that the man of God might be thoroughly equipped for every good work." 2Timothy 3: 16, 17.

God wrote the Book of Love, the Bible, for God is love. Every song writer looks for inspiration for a song. It can come from a joyous occasion or a time of grieving. It can be inspired by history or current events. The lyrics to this song which inspired lead singer of the Monotones who recorded this song, was the Pepsodent Toothpaste ad popular at this time in 1950s with a jingle, "you'll wonder where the yellow went, when you brush your teeth with Pepsodent."

The Bible describes itself as inspired by God. It was written over a 1500-year period by 40 different human authors in three different languages. One cannot imagine a more difficult, seemingly impossible way to construct a book or tell a story, much less it become the most famous, best-selling book of all times. Paul writing to Timothy tells us the authors were inspired by God. On what basis do we come to conclude this is an 'inspired by God' book?

Unity of Scripture. It is more than amazing—to write 66 books in three different languages by 40 different human authors centuries apart and they fit together. It had to come from an "outside editor and source"who guided the 1500-year project. *Accuracy* in facts. Dr. Luke records 32 countries, 54 cities, and 9 islands, all which existed then and now and are verified. *Prophecy*. Predictions made years and years before they happened exactly as predicted and are verified by multiple sources. I wonder Who, who wrote the Book of Love? God!

In the 21st century we discovered another book God wrote. It was mentioned over 3000 years ago by David who wrote in Psalm 139 where David records God was involved in his conception and formed him in his mother's womb. He writes: "Your eyes saw my substance, being yet unformed. And in Your *book* they all were written. The days fashioned for me when yet there was none of them." The assumption was David was using a metaphor to explain how God forms a human life in the womb from conception, not that there was really an actual book.

Fast forward to June of 2000. Location: The White House in Washington D.C. The human genome code, DNA of our species, the hereditary code of life had been broken. The newly revealed text was 3 billion letters long, written in a strange and cryptographic four-letter code. President Bill Clinton had gathered together the members of the team which had broken the code to celebrate this global project. Clinton recognized this accomplishment as ' the most wondrous map ever produced by mankind as we are learning the language in which God created life.' Dr. Frances Collins, head of the project said, "It's a humbling day for me, and awe-inspiring, to realize we have caught a glimpse of our own instruction *book*, previously only known to God."(The Language of God: A Scientist Presents Evidence for Belief. Dr. Francis S. Collins.) Now you know Who wrote the Book of Love.

The Book of Love

This song is an excellent example of the "doo-wop" sound which was popular in the late 1950s and early '60s. The song was written by lead singer, Charles Patrick of the Monotones. One of the distinctive sounds of the song was a "boom" sound which came entirely by accident. While rehearsing the song in their garage, a kid was kicking a ball against the garage. When they played it back, they liked the sound and left it in the song. They were one of the many local bands we all grew up with and later came to be called, "garage bands."

Sales took off and the small Mascot Record label could not keep up with demand. The record was re-issued on the Chess Record label and would go on to reach number 5 on the POP Chart and No. 3 on the R&B chart.

The Monotones are considered "one-hit wonders," as this was their only hit single. The song was performed by Sha Na Na at Woodstock in 1969. It was in the movies, "American Graffiti,"

"Christine," and "Stand By Me." The song is also referenced in Don McLean's classic, "American Pie."

Other popular "doo-wop" songs known for their harmonies were: "Duke of Earl," "Blue Moon," "The

Lion Sleeps Tonight," "Stay," and "16 Candles"—to mention a few.

"ONLY LOVE CAN BREAK A HEART, AND ONLY LOVE CAN MEND IT AGAIN"

"He, God, heals the brokenhearted and binds up their wounds." Psalm 147:3

This song, one of many hits, written by the team of Hal David (lyrics) and Burt Bacharach (music) went to number 2 on the charts recorded by Gene Pitney. Perhaps there are no lyrics which describe the heights and depths and confusion of love than this song. Love can break your heart. And love can mend it again. Are you noticing the fascination mankind has with this emotion we call , love? Love makes life worth living. It sets us apart from the rest of the creation.

God is love. His love is a perfect love which casts out fear. It is a true love. Love is the subject of the Bible. Love is the motivation which drew up the plan of salvation. It was grace, amazing grace which brought it down to man. For God so loved the world He gave His only begotten Son. Loving is about giving. "This is love: not that we loved God, but that He loved us and sent His Son as an atoning sacrifice for our sins."(I John 4: 10) I don't know about you—but that is crazy. Crazy, Sweet love. One can give without loving; but you cannot love without giving. When you love someone, you hurt when they hurt; rejoice, when they rejoice. What concerns me, concerns God. And God, we are told, can be grieved. Jesus wept with Mary and Martha at the tomb of Lazarus. He cried over Jerusalem.

Remember when you were first falling in love with your spouse? You thought of them constantly. Listen to this: God's thoughts toward you outnumber the grains of sand. "Oh, what manner of love is this the Father has lavished on us, that we might be called the children of God."(I John3: 1) Do you understand this truth? God longs for you. He wants to adopt you as His child in accordance with His pleasure and will. To those who believe He has given the authority to be called the children of God.

Jesus is therefore our true elder brother. I was lost. The Father sent Jesus to the far country to find me. I was blinded to the truth. I was dead in sin and trespasses. He brought me home. He brought me to the Father with great joy. Jesus said there was cheering in heaven when He brought me home.(Read Luke 15, the Prodigal Son.) There was a great celebration. Jesus is the life of the party and the love of my life.

Hal David and Burt Bacharach teamed up for many hit songs. The subject of love was often the theme. This love of God is perfect, true, giving, unconditional, everlasting, crazy and sweet. It's what the world needs now—the love of God shed abroad in our hearts. When we love someone, and they do not return our love it breaks our hearts. Has your heart been broken? "The Lord is close to the brokenhearted and saves those who are crushed in spirit."(Psalm 34: 18)

"Only Love Can Break a Heart"[6]

Burt Bacharach and Hal David were the most prolific writing team of hit songs from the late 1950s through the 1980s. 73 Top 40 hits in the USA. Bacharach was a six-time Grammy Award winner; three-time Academy Award winner. His songs were recorded by over 1000 artists, as diverse as: Marty Robbins, Sonny James, Perry Como and Barbara Streisand, Dionne Warwick, Richard Chamberlin, Dusty Springfield , and the list goes on to this day.

Sonny James took this song to #2 on the Billboard's Hot Country Singles in 1972, ten years after its first recording.

Gene Pitney's version went to #2 in the 1962 release. Pitney was a composer himself having written "Hello Mary Lou" a signature hit for Ricky Nelson and "Rubber Ball" a top hit for Bobby Vinton. Ironically, in 1962 when Only Love went to number 2 on Billboard, the number one hit was "He's a Rebel" recorded by the Chiffons and was written and composed by Gene Pitney. Pitney was composer and writer of the number 1 hit, and singer and recorder of the number 2 hit! What an amazing accomplishment.

---

[6] Written by: Burt Bacharach and Hal David. Recorded by: Gene Pitney. 1962—# 2 on Billboard Hits.

"WHAT THE WORD NEEDS NOW IS LOVE, SWEET LOVE"

"If I have the gift of prophecy and can fathom all mysteries and all knowledge and if I have faith that can move mountains, but HAVE NOT LOVE, I am nothing." (I Corinthians 13)

It is interesting in another mega Bacharach-David hit song, recorded by Jackie Deshannon, the lyricists by the second stanza is letting us know who they are asking for this sweet love is the Lord. Why? For God is the source of this type of love.

No wonder we are all looking for love. It was out of love God created the world. It is truly love which makes the world go around.

Man was made to be loved and to be a lover. When asked what the greatest commandment was, Jesus replied: The greatest commandment is to love the Lord your God with all your heart and with all your soul and with all your strength and with all your mind. And love your neighbor as yourself." (Luke 10) In fact Jesus said all the laws and prophets of the Bible rest on these two laws. When you factor in Jesus also told us to love our enemies—you realize if we could do these three things, they would solve most every problem.

Man looks on the outside. God investigates every human heart and sees what is there. He sees what is hidden there in the depths of our hearts. Jeremiah said the heart is deceitful above all things and desperately wicked, who can know it? The Lord can.

God judges the sin in our hearts. Can God be loving and judgmental? Yes. Moralizing is making a judgment but not being moved to do anything about it. Compassion is being moved to do something about it. We read in the Scriptures; Jesus was moved by compassion. The law was given by Moses, but grace and truth came by Jesus Christ. (John 1)

Listen to this beautiful verse and think of two lovers who have had a quarrel: "Mercy and truth are met together; righteousness and peace have kissed one another." Psalm 85. Mercy and forgiveness can only be shown toward someone by someone who has the power to punish or forgive. The prisoner can only be set free or punished by the law and law givers, which declared him guilty. He can receive a pardon and be set free or be executed. Judgement and love came together at the Cross of Calvary. It is for freedom which Christ set us free.

This love reveals itself in mutual, voluntary submission. This is a picture of the husband who loves his wife and desires the best for her and will sacrifice for her good. And it is true of the wife who wants the best for her husband and places his interests above her own. Parents do this for children. God has done it for us. He gave Himself. Sacrificed for our good, wanting the best for us. And God went first, knowing we may choose not to return HIs love.

And this love of God is the answer to the song writer's question of what the world needs now.

"What the Word Needs Now is Love, Sweet Love"[7]

Jackie DeShannon was born Sharon Lee Myers in Hazel, Kentucky. Her parents Sandra Jean and James Myers were a farming family who were musically talented. She loved country music from an early age and was singing country favorites by the age of six on the local radio. Her parents left farming and moved to Aurora, Illinois where her father worked as a barber. By age 11, she was appearing on local television. At age sixteen she appeared on Pee Wee King's popular Country and Western Television show. She left high school after her sophomore year and began to record under different names, finally settling on the name, Jackie DeShannon.

Her voice and interpretation of country and western standards caught the attention of rocker, Eddie Cochran, who introduced her to his singer-songwriter girlfriend, Shirley Sheely and they formed a successful song writing team. In March of 1965 she recorded "What the Word Needs Now"after the Bacharach-David song was turned down by Dionne

---

[7] Writers: Burt Bacharach and Hal David. Released: April 15, 1965. Recorded by Jackie DeShannon. Peaked at: # 7 in July 1965 on US Hot 100; reached #1 in Canada in the summer of 1965. Dionne Warwick turned this song down, saying it was "too country" for her taste. She did later record it on album, "Where is the Love."

Warwick. She dated Elvis Presley, made a couple of popular beach movies and toured with the Beatles. She enjoyed friendships with the Everly Brothers and Ricky Nelson. She wrote and recorded the hit song, "Put a Little Love in Your Heart." She also wrote and composed, Kim Carnes' major hit, "Bette Davis Eyes."

The writing team of Bacharach and David had worked their magic again. Hal David said they worked different ways. Sometimes he got the idea for lyrics and Burt provided the melody. Other times, Burt got the idea for a melody and Hal David came up with the lyrics. In this song, the lyrics and melody begin to come together in 1962. It was not until 1965 when Hal David came up with the lead in for the second stanza adding the word, Lord. "Lord, we don't need another mountain," that the song came together and was finished in two days.

What the world need now is love, sweet love and sometimes when we add the Lord into our song of life, it all comes together.

"YOU CAN'T HURRY LOVE"

"Love is patient." 1 Corinthians 13.

I agree what the world needs now is love, the sweet love of the Lord, which David said tasted like honey. But this Mo-Town hit by the Supremes tells us we can't hurry love; you just must wait for love. A wise mother had offered this advice to her daughter. You must be patient and wait. The lyrics also informed us the game of love was a game of give and take.

Time is a mystery. You cannot save it. You can spend it or invest it. If you are not careful you end up wasting it. It seemed in our youth; time passed too slowly sometimes as we watched the clock in the classroom waiting for the final bell to ring to get out of school. Christmas seemed to take forever to get here. Who couldn't wait to be sixteen and get their driver's license?

Now we are told to wait for love, not hurry it. Isn't it interesting to note the first miracle Jesus performed in the Gospel of John was at a wedding? The relationship of a Christian to the Lord Jesus is compared to a marriage. God chose this special union between a man and a woman to symbolize the relationship with Him. A marriage is two people living the same life together. The Church is called the Bride of Christ.

Consider the time taken in the steps of the traditional Jewish Wedding in the time of Jesus:

1. Betrothal: the groom travels from his father's house to the home of prospective bride. This betrothal would be considered in today's custom, the engagement.
2. The groom then returns to his father's house to prepare a place to live for him and his bride. This could take up to 12 months.
3. The groom comes for his bride when the building is complete at a time not exactly known.
4. The couple then return as husband and wife to the father's house to consummate the marriage and celebrate a wedding feast.

It was at this wedding feast, Jesus attended along with his disciples, and his mother is present. They run out of wine early in the celebration, and Jesus' mother informs Jesus of this problem. The miracle Jesus performed was to turn the water into wine. Wine has various meanings in the Bible, and one of them is the fullness of joy. Jesus is the life of the party. So: don't hurry love. And be sure to invite Jesus as the most honored guest to your wedding. Marriage is often referred to as "tying the knot." When Jesus is the center of the marriage, you have a three-fold cord which is not easily broken. If you do this—this love you waited for will keep you together.

"You Can't Hurry Love"[8]

The Supremes would be one of the top girl music groups of the '60s. This song was one of the many successful Motown releases. It would become the Supremes 7th number one hit. In September of 1966 the Supremes performed this hit song on the Ed Sullivan show.

Barry Gordy was the president of Motown Records. In 1967, he renamed the group: Diana Ross and the Supremes. They had started out in 1959, known as the Primettes. They formed the Primettes as a sister act to the Primes, which featured Paul Williams and Eddie Kendricks, who went on to form the Temptations. As the Supremes they had 12 number one hits.

Diana Ross gave her final performance with the Supremes on January 14, 1970. The Supremes' story was made into a move entitled: "Sparkle." The group

---

[8] Recorded by: The Supremes with lead singer Diana Ross. Recorded on: The Motown Record Label. Released: Summer of 1966. Written by Holland-Dozier-Holland. Peaked at: #1 on Billboard Pop Singles; #5 on UK charts. Re-released: 1983 by Phil Collins reaching #1 in UK and #10 in USA. The Motown sound was a mix of gospel, R& B and pop music. This song was inspired by the Gospel song, "You Can't Hurry God, He's Right on Time," written by Dorothy Love Coates of the Original Gospel Harmonettes.

was also the inspiration of the Tony Award-winning musical, "Dreamgirls," which ran on Broadway for 1522 performances.

Love was often the theme of their songs, including "Stop in the Name of Love," "Love is Like an Itching in My Heart," and "Baby, I Need Your Love."

"CAN'T BUY ME LOVE"

"For the love of money is a root of all kinds of evil."(2 Timothy 6)

Even those mop-top boys from England, the Beatles, who changed the hair styles for a whole generation had discovered money can't buy you love.

I don't know about you, but I love stories and movies about buried treasure. Treasure and treasures represent something of great value and worth to us. "Treasure Island" and "The Count of Monte Cristo" come to mind as two of my favorite books and movies. What memorable characters and adventures are brought together to weave the most wonderful stories. In the movie, "Count of Monte Cristo," the treasure Edmund Dantes finds is enormous and of such extravagance and wealth, his servant carries a wagon load to purchase the castle of his dreams. Yet the hatred which drove Dantes to revenge, made him miserable. He said, "The wretched and the miserable should turn to their Savior first—yet they do not hope in Him, until all hope is gone."(*The Count of Monte Cristo*, by Alexander Dumas.)

Here is what Jesus said about treasure. "Lay not up treasure for yourself on earth, where moth and rust corrupt and thieves break into steal. Lay up treasures for yourself in heaven, where neither rust or moth corrupt nor thieves break into steal." Don't miss this truth, for herein lies the treasure principle.

" For where your treasure is there will be your heart also."(Matthew 6) Did you notice the treasure is for yourself? Jesus went on to say, "No man can serve two masters. Either he will hate the one and love the other or will be devoted to the one and despise the other. You cannot serve both God and money." Jim Elliot who was killed by the tribe he was trying to minister to said, "A man is no fool to give up what he cannot keep, in order to gain what he can never lose."

There are more quotes about love than perhaps any other word in any language. Yet it sometimes remains indescribable. Listen to these truths about love:

"You can always give without loving, but you can never love without giving." Amy Carmichael.

"Being loved is life's second greatest blessing; loving is the greatest." Jack Hyles

"For God so loved the world, He gave His Only Begotten Son that whosoever should believe in Him would never perish, but have everlasting love." Jesus Christ. Why did Jesus advise us to lay up our treasure in heaven? Because we were made for a person and a place. We get a little glimpse of heaven when we fall in love with the right person in the right way. God gave us the ability to love and be loved as the greatest treasure we could possess. Jesus said a man's life does not exist in the abundance of his possessions. The person we were made for is Jesus. The place we were made for-is heaven. Are you on a treasure hunt? There is a map which guides you to the most extravagant buried treasure. It is called the Bible. It will guide you to a treasure more precious than all the gold. Love is the greatest treasure of all, but the Beatles were right, money can't buy you love. It's not for sale.

"Can't Buy Me Love"[9]

This song was also included in the Beatles' "Hard Days Night" Album. This record was finished and recorded first in the EMI Studios in Paris, France, where the Beatles were performing 18 days of sold-out concerts at the Olympia Theater. They returned to EMI Studios, Abby Lane, London on February 25, 1964 to finish overdubs.

The song was written in Paris under pressure to release a follow-up hit "I Want to Hold Your Hand." This song was their third number one single in a row, following their first two, respectively: "I Want to Hold Your Hand" and "She Loves You."

When "Can't Buy Me Love" reached number 1, the Beatles held the entire top five on the Hot 100. No other act has ever held the top five spots simultaneously.

The writing team of Lennon and McCartney were a phenomenon. The vocals were shared by all four Beatles: John, Paul, George and Ringo. They not only

---

[9] Composers: John Lennon and Paul McCartney. Recorded by: The Beatles. Released: March 1964. Reached: Number 1 on April 4, 1964

changed hair styles, they led the way for the British invasion. A new chapter in Rock and Roll had begun.

We later discovered one of the Beatles' influences was Jackson, Tennessee's hometown Rock-a -Billy pioneer, Carl Perkins. Music can span time and space.

"HOW DEEP IS YOUR LOVE?"

"For I am persuaded that neither death nor life, nor angels, nor principalities, nor powers, nor things present, nor things to come, nor height nor depth, nor any other created thing can separate us from the love of God which is in Christ Jesus, our Lord. "Romans 8: 38, 39.

The Bee Gees, the Gibbs brothers, had numerous hits in the '70s in the disco era. This song was featured on their album from the movie "Saturday Night Fever." John Travolta showed us his dancing skills against the backdrop of a movie with a common theme. Travolta's character is a young man still living at home with his parents. He has a job as a clerk in a paint store. The only thing he looks forward to is Saturday night and dancing. He and his friends are restless and sometimes violent. Dancing is Travolta's only real joy. His desire is to escape the life he is living. Something is missing and so the search for meaning and purpose begins.

God stated it clearly and simply when he said this about Adam: "It is not good that man should be alone; I will make him a helpmate. Therefore, a man shall leave his father and mother and be joined to his wife, and they shall become one flesh." Genesis 2. Our relationship with Jesus is compared to a marriage, because we are joined together with Him as in a marriage with two people living the same life.

We are told what the world needs now is love. It's the missing ingredient. But we can't hurry love, we have to be patient. Now we are told we cannot buy love. It's not for sale. And now we are questioned about the depth of love. The verses we quoted in the beginning tell us nothing or no one can ever separate us from the love of Christ.

Life is about relationships. Relationships take work, give and take, sacrifice, and placing others' needs before our own. If we are not careful our relationships can drift apart. Love is the anchor which will hold the marriage together. Storms come, but the anchor holds if the love is deep.

Corrie Ten Boom in the horrific, hellish pit of a Nazi Concentration Camp said: "There is no pit so deep that God is not deeper still." (from the movie, *The Hiding Place*) How deep is your love?

"How Deep Is Your Love?"[10]

This hit song replaced Debby Boone's "You Light Up My Life" which had held the number one position for six weeks.

"How Deep Is Your Love" was Barry Gibb's favorite song. It was rated as number 325 of the top 500 hits of all times by Rolling Stone. The Gibbs

------

[10] Written and Recorded by: The Bee Gees. Year Released: 1977 (Part of soundtrack of "Saturday Night Fever"). Reached No. 1 on Billboard 100 in December of 1977. Would become the first of six consecutive number one hits by the Bee Gees.

brothers, Barry, Maurice and Robin did most of the writing and composing.

Barry's falsetto voice was usually the lead vocal in all the Bee Gees' songs. Robin and Maurice were fraternal twins and younger brother Andy had a successful solo career. Barry is the only surviving brother. A truly musical family who were identified with the disco era as memorialized in film with John Travolta's dazzling dance routine.

"I WANT TO HOLD YOUR HAND"

"Unless I see in His hands the print of the nail, and put my finger into the print of the nails, and put my hands into His side, I will not believe."(Thomas the Apostle, John 20:25)

Thomas became known as "Doubting Thomas." All of us have experienced doubts about something, a feeling of uncertainty. Sometimes, in Thomas's case, something sounds too good to be true. We don't want to get our hopes up and then be disappointed. Doubt usually occurs when we are confronted with the unknown, the uncertain and the yet, unseen.

I recall my grandson, Jack, when he was a little boy slipping his hand into mine as we started up a dark stairway. He was waiting for the light to be turned on and dispel the darkness. The world culture skeptically says, 'I will believe it when I see it.' Jesus said, if you believe, then you will see. Jesus told Thomas on that day He appeared to him: "Blessed are those who have not seen, yet believed." We are all afraid of something, real, imagined and/or unknown.

But by placing his hand in my hand, Little Jack placed his faith in his granddaddy. His hand in my hand gave him a link to someone he trusted and believed could take care of the unknown and the unseen. Remember when you had such faith in your parents? You believed they could take care of any problem. This is the child-like faith the enemy wants to sever with doubt. And when doubt is not dealt with it can grow into unbelief like a cancer.

"Now faith is being sure of what we hope for and certain of what we do not see."(Hebrews 11: 1) Faith is putting your hand in the hand of the Master who stilled the sea. Faith connects you to the Light of the world when all is dark.

Feed your faith and doubt will starve. However, feed your doubts and faith will starve. We must stand on the promises of God. And when you are standing on those promises reach out and take His hand. In the Gospel song, "Put Your Hand In the Hand," the second stanza tells us a key: "My momma taught me how to pray before I reached the age of seven. When I'm down on my knees, that's when I'm closest to heaven."

Our granddaughter, Virginia asked her grandmother "Gin-Gin, do you only pray at meals and bedtime?" Gin-Gin told her, "You can pray anytime. And when you pray, the Lord Jesus says to everyone in heaven, 'Be quiet, Virginia wants to talk to me.'"

Tell Him the next time you are afraid, worried or doubtful, pray: "Lord Jesus, I want to hold your hand." He's closer than you think. He is just a prayer away.

"I Want to Hold Your Hand"[11]

When the Beatles appeared on Ed Sullivan on February 9, 1964, 73 million people tuned in that Sunday evening. It would become a moment many of us boomers remember, just as the moment we first heard President Kennedy had been shot. Their dress, their mop-hair styles, their accents were something new and different. Beatlemania had begun in earnest and would only grow larger.

They would have seven number one hits that year, all written by Lennon and McCartney. We were introduced to the foursome, George, Paul, John and Ringo. Three thousand fans were waiting for their arrival at the airport. They were immediately whisked off to a press conference. One reporter asked the Beatles, "How do you find America?"Ringo, the drummer answered: "We turned left at Greenland."Some critics said they were a gimmick and would not last long. Today only two of the Beatles survive, Paul McCartney and Ringo Starr.

---

[11] Written by John Lennon & Paul McCartney. Recorded by the Beatles in October 1963. In the UK, the song went to number 2 the day it was released. The only reason it did not go to number 1, is the Beatles; "She Loves Me"was still number one. . Released in USA in January of 1964 and reached number 1 on Billboard, February 1st. It was also the first record to use four-track technology.

John Lennon was murdered outside his apartment and George Harrison died of cancer.

The Beatles closed their set in NYC that Sunday night on February 9th, 1964 with: "I Want to Hold Your Hand." It was 79 days after President Kennedy was assassinated. For the second time that school year we had all gathered together around a television in our college dormitory to watch something which was of great interest. What a different atmosphere from when we gathered to watch the aftermath of the assassination of Kennedy. It seemed as if our period of mourning had ended. Maybe this explains why their songs are so memorable to us.

"MY LIFE"

"The words of the Teacher, son of David, king in Jerusalem: Meaningless! Meaningless! Utterly meaningless! Everything is meaningless!" (Ecclesiastes 1: 1&2)

These written words of King Solomon are clear, aren't they? What is going on? Was he having a bad day? No, he was surveying his life. A king who had wisdom, wealth and women. Solomon built palaces and gardens with all the décor and trappings of a mansion right out of Southern Living magazine. As a wealthy king he lived as if it were as an ongoing episode of Lifestyles of the Rich and Famous. Yet in his life, in all his accomplishments King Solomon could find no meaning or purpose, nothing which satisfied a longing in his heart. You know why that is? It is because God placed a longing for eternity in our hearts. Which means the "here and now" does not have the ability to give my life or yours meaning and purpose. Without discovering the meaning and purpose of life, we will always have a void in our lives. We were created by God and for God.

Now let me provide you with what King Solomon learned in the end: "Now all has been heard; here is the conclusion of the matter: Fear God and keep His commandments, for this is the whole duty of man."(Eccl. 12: 13 NIV) This is advice from a man known for his wisdom. He is telling you how to invest your life for the only outcome which not only satisfies you but enriches you. If you were an investor and Warren Buffett told you he could show you how to become wealthy. You would listen to him, wouldn't you? You would be wise to heed his advice. King Solomon was a man known for his wisdom.

I cannot help but think Billy Joel's song, "My Life" is autobiographical. To me it sounds like a letter or conversation I had with my parents when they were trying to get me to come home, because I had chosen to live my life in a way which they thought was wrong.

Warren Buffett credited his success to his reading habits. He spends 80% of his time reading and thinking, meditating on what he has read. Buffett said knowledge is like compound interest, it builds up. Psalm 1 says the man who delights in the word of God and meditates in it day and night will be like a tree planted by the rivers of water that brings forth its fruit in season, whose leaf shall not wither and whatever he does will succeed. The Bible contains the mind of God. Read it to be wise. Believe it to be saved. Practice it to be holy. It will direct your path.

It can change your life. It can give your life meaning. I know because it changed – MY LIFE!

"My Life"[12]

The opening lines about a comedian who sold everything and moved to the West Coast to become a comedian are said to be about comedian Richard Lewis.

It also resonates with all of us who in our youth went out to discover our way in life, finding what would satisfy our souls and provide our lives with meaning. Billy Joel was a talented, classically trained pianist.

Regionally, he played in Memphis at Overton Square for a season and soon he was playing to standing room only crowds. The Piano Man was on his way.

Phil Ramone was an engineer, producer and violinist whose list of stars he worked with read like a "who's who" list of accomplished superstars. A dinner with him after Joel's first concert at Carnegie Hall resulted in their first album, "Stranger."

Billy Joel later said of Ramone: "If I hadn't met Phil Ramone, I would have had an entirely different life."

I can say the same about the Lord Jesus. If I had not met Him on the balcony of a 10th floor hotel in

---

[12] Written and performed by Billy Joel. Released as single 1978. Charts: Number 2 on Adult Contemporary List; Number 3 on Billboard Hot 100. Included on the Album: "Stranger," with producer, Phil Ramone.

Nashville, I would have had an entirely different life. The disciples met a 'stranger' on the road to Emmaus. The 'stranger' turned out to be the resurrected Lord Jesus. Their hearts burned within them as they realized, He was alive. Don't let Him be a stranger to you. He wants to have dinner with you and change your life. "Behold I stand at the door and knock, and if anyone hears my voice and opens the door, I will come in and dine with him and he with Me."(Rev. 3: 20)

I am so glad I let Him in, and He has not just become a part of my life, He is my life.

"(YOUR LOVE KEEPS LIFTING ME) HIGHER AND HIGHER"

"And I, if I am lifted up from the earth, will draw all peoples to Myself." John 12: 32, Jesus speaking.

It is not uncommon to see the love and devotion for another person make one strive to do their best for them. This type of love has the potential to keep lifting one's life higher and higher. I believe this type of love takes our eyes off ourselves and puts them on another. Think of the songs which involve the eyes: "The Look of Love" I Only Have Eyes for You"; "My Eyes Adored You"; "Just One Look, That's All it Took."

The great preacher, C. A. Spurgeon recounts his conversion experience as a 15-year old and his deep sense of need for deliverance. Because of a snowstorm, he ended up that snowy Sunday morning in a Primitive Methodist Church. The regular preacher had been unable to get to the church and an un-prepared layman stepped in to preach that morning. His text was Isaiah 45: 22: "Look to Me, and be saved, all you ends of the earth! For I am God and there is no other."

The man went on to say: 'it ain't lifting your foot or your finger, it is just look. You may be the biggest fool, and yet you can look. You are looking at yourselves. No use looking there you will never find comfort in yourselves."He went on to explain we are to look up at Christ lifted on the cross. See Him there sweating great drops of blood, gasping for air, bleeding from His wounds and pleading for our forgiveness. The man then looked up in the gallery at young Spurgeon and said, "Young man, you look most miserable. And you will always be miserable in life and in death. Look to Jesus Christ." Spurgeon said it was as if the clouds had rolled back and the darkness rolled away. It was at that moment when his eyes beheld the Lord Jesus lifted for his sins, he was saved. And his love for his Savior kept lifting him up, higher and higher for the rest of his life.

Jackie Wilson said in this song until this love came into his life, he had only known disappointments and heartaches. But when this love came into his life those emotions were replaced by a love which kept lifting him higher and higher.

Are you down-hearted today? Has life disappointed you? Then look to Jesus. Invite Him in and find what your heart has been searching for by simply looking up at the cross at the One who loves you with an everlasting love. I promise you this love will lift you higher and higher, until one day it will lift you all the way to heaven, to a heavenly home prepared for you. Jesus is the Divine Magnet. Just look, really look, and be lifted up higher and higher.

"Higher and Higher"[13]

Jackie Wilson first sang it as a ballad in the recording session. Carl Davis told him that was wrong, he had to "jump on it"and go with the percussion. Wilson then cut the lead vocal in one take.

Jackie Wilson was a tenor with a four-octave range. He was considered a master showman and his nickname was, "Mr. Excitement." Jackie began singing as youth, accompanying his mother in the church choir. Jackie probably got his musical genes from her as she possessed a beautiful voice. Jackie also began drinking at an early age which caused him to be sent to a detention facility in Lansing twice.

However, through perseverance and good management, Wilson's career continued to flourish. His dancing, dress style and enthusiasm influenced James Brown and Michael Jackson. Elvis Presley was also an admirer of Wilson, and they later became good friends. In fact, Elvis's throwing used handkerchiefs was copied from Wilson's throwing of his bow ties into the audience.

---

[13] Written by Gary Jackson and Carl Smith. Recorded by Jackie Wilson. Released: 1967. Charts: Number 1 on Billboard R&B; Number 6 on Billboard Hot 100. Recorded at Columbia studios in Chicago and used the Funk Brothers as back up for the session.

In 1975, in the middle of singing "Lonely Teardrop," Wilson suffered a massive heart attack. He slipped into a coma. After a brief recovery in 1976, Jackie Wilson slipped back into a semi-comatose state in which he would linger until 1984 when he died at age 49.

"A NATURAL WOMAN"

"Peace I leave with you. My peace I give to you; not as the world gives do, I give to you. Let not your heart be troubled, neither let it be afraid." John 14:27

Now if you are wondering how this devotional connects to the mega hit of Aretha Franklin's recording of the Carole King song, "A Natural Woman," you must read the lyrics. Just as we are told all Scripture is inspired, writers of songs look for inspiration also. The writer of this classic Franklin hit may have been experiencing lack of inspiration. Read or listen to the lyrics and see the progression of the rhyme: uninspired, tired, unkind, mind. Regardless of gender we have all had those types of days the writer describes. But then comes the good news: someone who brought peace of mind and changed their outlook of life and how they felt. (You Make Me Feel Like) A Natural Woman, lyrics ©Sony/ATV Music

Aretha Franklin was called, rightfully so, the "Queen of Soul." Her father was a famous preacher, C. L. Franklin and she grew up singing in his church. But these lyrics describe an emptiness, a longing for some thing or someone to fill a void. Life is uninspired, tired with no peace of mind. Knowing her background, I can see Ms. Franklin turning this song into a prayer during trying times.

Romans 5 tells us we have peace with God. But the verse in John 14 says we have the peace of none other than the Lord Jesus Christ. It is like a prayer went up: 'Lord I am so tired; I cannot face another day.' And then the answer came in the person of the Lord Jesus Christ who gave us His peace. A peace which passes understanding. The key to your peace of mind. "He has the key of David, He who opens, and no one shuts, and shuts and no one opens."Revelation 3: 8.

Stories are the language of the heart. And once set to music they arouse our senses and contact our souls. And Aretha was the Queen of Soul. Whether it is Jackie Wilson recalling the days he was down hearted and disappointed or Eric Clapton grieving for his son who was in heaven. Man has been using music as an outlet for his emotions since the dawn of time. One of the greatest songwriters of all times was King David. God saw the need for songs, therefore He put 150 songs in the middle of the Bible. The Top 150!

And here is how He ended those 150 songs with a full orchestra: "Praise Him with the sound of the trumpets; Praise Him with the lute and harp! Praise Him with the timbrel and dance; Praise Him with stringed instruments and flutes! Praise Him with the loud cymbals; Praise with clashing cymbals! Let everything that has breath praise the Lord! (Psalm 150)

God knows what is missing in your life. He knows how to fill that void, inspire your life and give you peace which passes understanding. He will put a new song in your heart.

(You Make Me Feel Like) "A Natural Woman"[14]

This song would become one of Aretha's signature songs. By the end of the 1960s she was known as the "Queen of Soul." Her father, C. L. Franklin, was a noted Baptist preacher whose sermons were well known. His powerful voice gave him the nickname of the "man with the million-dollar voice." His church in Detroit, where they moved when Aretha was just a child was frequently visited by leading politicians, Martin Luther King, Gospel singer, James Cleveland, entertainers, Sam Cooke and Jackie Wilson. Aretha's mother played piano and was an accomplished vocalist.

This song uses a technique often used in creating a song, a story set to music. It is a before and after story. The song writer starts the song by telling us how life was before she met this person and how life was after she met this person. We visualize the heroine of the song looking out her window at the morning rain and describing her life before she met this life-changing person. The description of her life tells the story: uninspired, tired of an existence in which the world seemed so unkind. Then comes a person who changes everything and the song soars as the life of this woman soars. We are told in the

---

[14] Written by Carole King & Gerry Goffin. Recorded by Aretha Franklin. Charts: Reached #8 on Billboard Hot 100.

lyrics whom this person is in the opening stanza, the Lord. The One who is the key to our peace of mind. For me there was life before I met the Lord, a life lived in search of meaning. A life which was void of meaning. A life which was unkind. My life changed the day His life came into my life.

Aretha Franklin would chart 112 singles on the Billboard Hot 100. She would have 20 number 1 hits on Billboard R&B. She would win numerous awards in her career. One of her most amazing performances occurred in 1998 at the Grammy Awards. Opera star, Luciano Pavarotti was scheduled to sing "Nessun Dorma" but cancelled at the last moment after the show had already started. Aretha filled in with no rehearsal and nailed it.

In 2015, she sang "Natural Woman" at the Kennedy Center in honor of Carole King who was being honored and was also the writer of "Natural Woman." Aretha was 73 years old, and in poor health. Google the performance and watch her bring the audience to their feet and move President Obama to tears. She looked out that night and was inspired. She was not tired. She was at peace with the talent God had given her. One of her all-time best-selling albums was a collection of gospel classics entitled—"Amazing Grace." She was an amazing talent.

"IF YOU WANNA BE HAPPY FOR THE REST OF YOUR LIFE"

"Blessed (happy) are the poor in spirit, for theirs is the kingdom of God. Blessed (happy) are those who mourn, for they shall be comforted. Blessed (happy) are the meek, for they shall inherit the earth. Blessed (happy) are those who hunger and thirst for righteousness for they shall be filled. "Jesus goes on to say those who show mercy, who are pure in heart, peacemakers and the persecuted, will be blessed. (Matthew 5, the Sermon on the Mount)

I have chosen this Jimmy Soul number 1 hit from 1963 for two reasons. First, I graduated from Peabody High School in 1963 and if you had asked me or any of my classmates what we wanted from life; we would have probably said to "be happy." The second reason I chose this song was because its recommendation of what one should do to be happy was the opposite of what most people would consider happiness. The song expressed a personal point of view for sustaining happiness. The writer believed marrying a pretty woman would cause you problems, whereas marrying an unattractive woman would make one happy.

Jesus tells us what will make us happy, and it is the opposite of what our society and culture tells us will make us happy. Now let's be clear about the word—"happy." Happy is an emotion which is usually dependent on outward circumstances being favorable. Joy is something which comes from within and brings peace and contentment. Contentment must be learned. Poverty of any kind would not be viewed by our culture as favorable. This culture does not want to mourn over sin; nor does it celebrate the meek but celebrates the bold, the beautiful, the winners not losers. Yet Jesus said exactly the opposite—blessed are the poor, the meek those who mourn and are persecuted.

"If any would be first, he must first be last of all and servant to all." (Mark 9: 35)

"After that, He(Jesus) poured water into a basin and begin to wash the disciple's feet, drying them with the towel that was wrapped around Him." Later, He said: "Do you understand what I have done? I have set an example for you that you should do as I have done. Now that you know these things, you will be blessed (happy) if you do them."(John 13, the Last Supper)

So, if you wanna be happy for the rest of your life—you can follow Jimmy Soul's personal point of view. Or you can follow the Lord Jesus' personal point of view.

I will follow Jesus.

"If You Wanna Be Happy"[15]

Jimmy Soul was born James Louis McCleese. in North Carolina in 1942. As was often the case in the lives of these performers, he first began performing in church. Young Jimmy preached and sang as a youth. He was discovered by Frank Guida, who was known for producing what was called the "Norfolk Sound."Frank handled Gary U.S. Bonds who had already had several hits songs. Frank favored the calypso style and picked this song for his young protégé, now going by the name of Jimmy Soul. The song was influenced by a calypso song, "Ugly Woman."

Jimmy Soul became one of those performers who would be known as a "one-hit wonder." Failing to have a follow up hit, Soul joined the army. He fell into drug use later and in 1986 was sentenced to a prison term of 4 ½ to 9 years as a second offender. Soul would die at the age of 45 of a heart attack in 1988.

Happiness as described by the world's opinion is temporary and conditional. The joy of the Lord is neither. Like His peace, this joy passes understanding and produces contentment. The Westminster Catechism states: "The chief end of man is to glorify

---

[15] Written by: Joseph Royster, Carmella Guida and Frank Guida. Recorded by: Jimmy Soul on S.P.Q.R./London Records. Reached Number 1: May 18, 1963.

God and enjoy Him forever." Do you want to be happy for the rest of your life? In my personal point of view this Westminster Catechism captures exactly what makes life worth living and produces joy unspeakable.

"WHAT KIND OF FOOL DO YOU THINK I AM?"

"The fool has said in his heart there is no God." Psalm 14:1

Fool is defined as a person lacking in judgement. The Bible calls a fool, "senseless." A fool is also described as someone who disregards God's Word. Fools tend not to learn lessons from their mistakes, which is what this 1964 hit by the Tams is all about.

Other songs used the word "fool, fools or foolish" in their titles. The Tams had another hit song in 1968 entitled: "Be Young, Be Foolish, and Be Happy." Coincidently they also had another hit entitled: "I've Been Hurt" as fools are often hurt by foolish decisions. Other songs using this word are: "Why Do Fools Fall in Love?" and "Fools Rush In." Certainly, when we were young, we did foolish things, not thinking of the potential harm it could cause. The opposite of foolishness is wisdom. Wisdom is the ability to use your knowledge and experience to make wise decisions. Wisdom is different than knowledge. You have probably heard someone described as an "educated fool." Knowledge is information gained through experience, study and reasoning. Knowledge can exist without wisdom. Example: you can know how to use a gun; wisdom is knowing when to use it.

The Book of Proverbs is the best place to learn biblical wisdom. Knowledge knows the 10 Commandments, wisdom obeys them. In school, you gained knowledge. You were then tested to see if you could apply that knowledge in the right way. In life, tests come in a variety of ways. Sometimes in a test we are told to stand still; other times we are told to flee. We are told if we lack wisdom, we can ask God, and He will give it to us liberally. The way of wisdom is passed down from generation to generation. All of us are expected to get wisdom and to pass it on to the next generation.

Perhaps one of the most well-known quotes in modern Christendom is from Jim Elliot, the missionary killed by the very natives he was trying to share Christ with. He said, "A man is no fool, to give up what he cannot keep for that which he can never lose." Lay up treasure in heaven and you can enjoy it forever. Jesus understands the power of self-interest. He came to enlighten our self-interest as to what would best satisfy us. He enlightens because He is the Light of the World. He came to testify to the truth. He is the way, the truth and the life.

A man who got saved later in his life wanted to be an effective witness. He traveled every day to work by train and passed and encountered hundreds of people every day. He carried a brief case on which he wrote in large letters on one side: "I AM A FOOL FOR CHRIST." On the other side in large letters he wrote: Whose Fool Are You? God has chosen the foolish things of the world to confound the wise.

What kind of fool do you think I am?

"What Kind of Fool Do You Think I Am?"[16]

The Tams got their name from the tam hats they wore. They were a popular club band and toured the college circuit and concerts with founder Charles Pope until 2009, when he retired. The group still tours to this day

Jimmy Buffett was a big fan of their music and style.

They had hits in 1965, "I've Been Hurt" and, in 1968, "Be Young, Be Foolish, and Be Happy." The Tams were also popular in the U.K.

The Muscle Shoals Sound was a distinctive sound in the fast-changing styles of the 1960s. The Carolina Beach Sound was associated with a popular dance , "The Shag."

The Tams began performing in local taverns and nightclubs for $1.25 each. The Tams continue to tour and play up to 300 days per year with their backup band called, "14-K Gold." Their founder, Charles Pope, started the group with his brother, Joe. He always wanted their sound to be in perfect pitch. He stepped away from the microphone in 2009 and died in 2013 at age 76.

---

[16] Written by: Ray Whitley. Recorded in Muscle Shoals, Alabama at the FAME studio. Genre: R&B and Carolina Beach Music. Recorded by: The Tams 1964. Reached: Number 1 on Cash Box and # 9 Billboard Hot 100.

"NOWHERE MAN"

"There is a way which seems right to man, but its way ends in death."Proverbs14:12 says, "Enter by the narrow gate; for wide is the gate and broad is the way that leads to destruction, and there are many who go in by it. Because narrow is the gate and hard is the way which leads to life, and there are few who find it." Matthew 7: 13, 14. Where are you headed?

My college roommate, Max had the Rubber Soul album from the Beatles which contained this song. The lyrics of the Beatles' songs would often create discussions as to their meaning. Here the lyrics written by John Lennon started out with writer's block. Exhausted and trying to meet a deadline for a new album, Lennon had run out of ideas. He remembers falling to sleep thinking, I'm getting nowhere. The thought became a song. To a couple of college students trying to figure out life, it seemed to speak to our situation.

Ever ask someone where they were going and they replied, "Nowhere, man." Or in the '60s we might have said, "I am going with the flow." The principle of drifting is we not only drift *from* something or somewhere but also to something or somewhere. Do you have the feeling you are drifting through life?

There are different seasons in life. We are told to train up a child in the way he/she is to go and when they are old, they will not depart from it. I have seen this truth in my children and in my own life. We wanted to make sure we got our children headed in the right direction, to the good life. A life not wasted on the wrong things. Jesus said, "One's life does not consist in the abundance of the things he possesses." (Luke 12: 15) And then Jesus told a parable of a rich man whose ground yielded plentifully. He thought to himself, 'what shall I do, since I have no room to store my crops? He decided to expand. Then having finished the expansion project, sat back and said, "Now I am in good shape and can take it easy. Eat, drink and be merry." "But God said to him, "You fool! This night your soul will be required of you; then whose will those things be which you have provided?" (Luke 12: 16-19)

Ask yourself this question: "What is the one, single most important thing in your life? And if you get this wrong, where are you headed?" Nowhere, man.

"For whoever desires to save his life will lose it, and whoever loses his life for My sake and the gospel's will save it." Perhaps you are climbing the ladder of success but find when it is all over—you leaned your ladder against the wrong wall.

The Beatles pleaded with the nowhere man to please listen and told him you don't know what you are missing. Jesus said, "Anyone who has ears, let him hear." There is a difference between having ears and having ears to hear. Some hear the Word of God and do not allow it to take root because the world's pleasures drown it out. Please listen. You can miss heaven by 18 inches, the distance from your ears to your heart.

"Nowhere Man"[17]

The Beatles were exhausted from touring, Beatlemania and the controversy. John Lennon had stirred up with his comment: "we are more popular than Jesus Christ."

This song reflected Lennon's philosophical thinking and was the first song the Beatles had written that did not feature a boy-girl relationship and love.

Lennon later said, the song was about him. His marriage was failing. Beatlemania was insane. And the pressure to produce hit after hit was draining them. For guitar aficionados the guitar solo was recorded in unison with both John and George on their identical Sonic Blue Fender Stratocasters.

It was a busy time for the group in October of 1965. Not only were they writing and recording, they received the British MBE from Queen Elizabeth at Buckingham Palace the same week. MBE stands for: Member of the Most Excellent Order of the British Empire. This is given to an individual for outstanding

---

[17] Written by: John Lennon. Recorded by: The Beatles 1965 on Rubber Soul Album. Released in US in 1966. Reached: #3 on US Billboards Hot 100;Reached #2 on US Cash Box 100; and #1 on US Record World Top 100 Pops.

service to the community. In September of 1969, John Lennon privately told the other Beatles he was leaving. The official announcement was made on April 10, 1970. On the evening of December 8, 1980, John Lennon was shot and killed outside his apartment in NYC. He was 40 years old. I cried when I heard the news.

"BLOWING IN THE WIND"

"The wind blows where it wishes, and you hear the sound of it, but cannot tell where it comes from and where it goes. So is everyone who is born of the Spirit." (John 3: 8)

If the nowhere man was looking for an answer, Bob Dylan would tell him it was blowing in the wind. Peter, Paul and Mary recorded the hit version of this song. It burst onto the scene in the fall of 1963, and America was introduced to Bob Dylan who wrote this song. It was the beginning of an era when the Baby Boomers were headed to college, coming of age and asking more questions to which there seemed to be no answers.

Bob Dylan asked the question in this song about the number of times a man must look at the sky before he sees it. Interesting question; and he was not the first to ask it. There was another song writer years and years ago who wrote songs which asked thought-provoking questions. His name was David, the shepherd boy who would grow up to be a king. Looking up at the night sky while probably tending his sheep, David wrote; "When I consider Your heavens, the work of Your fingers, the moon, the stars, which you have ordained, what is man that you are mindful of him? And the son of man that you should visit him?" (Psalm 8) And again in Psalm 19 we read: "The heavens declare the glory of God; and the firmament show His handiwork. Day unto day utters speech. And night unto night reveals knowledge. There is no speech nor language where their voice is not heard."

God the Creator has revealed Himself to us in two witnesses. An external witness: creation. And an internal witness our conscience which bears witness to us what is right and wrong, good and evil. "Because what may be known of God is manifest in them, for God has shown it to them." (Romans 1: 19) Man is without excuse.

The most popular theory of our universe's origin centers on a cosmic event of unmeasured magnitude. The cosmic event which caused the creation of the universe is called "The Big Bang." With the invention of the Hubble telescope and its observations of galaxies the theory received more verification. Another breakthrough was the discovery of cosmic microwave radiation. Here is the bottom line: If there was a big bang, there had to be a Big Banger.

As far as the wind blowing, realize we are rotating at 1,000 miles per hour on our axis, while revolving around the sun at speeds up to 60,000 miles per hour. Dylan may have been right—the answer is blowing in the wind, or rather the One who is the source of the winds which blow where they might.

"Blowing in the Wind"[18]

I witnessed this trio's performance with an acoustic guitar and a stand-up bass as I watched their flawless performance of this song in the auditorium of Murray State College in Murray, Kentucky, in the fall of 1963.

We were the generation who would welcome 21-year-old Bob Dylan a folk singer who had been influenced by Woody Guthrie and Pete Seeger.

This song was not so much a protest song as some of Dylan's later songs would be, but more of a spiritual song which seemed to resonate with the times which were changing.

Bob Dylan would perform this song in 1997 at a Catholic Congress. Pope John Paul II was in attendance and told the crowd of 300,000 young Italian Catholics that the answer was indeed in the "wind," the wind of the Holy Spirit who would lead them to Jesus Christ.

Bob Dylan was another phenomenal talent who appeared in the 1960s just as the largest demographic group, the Baby Boomers were coming of age. We continued to change the culture around us, and question authority, and why things were the way they were. We were searching for answers to difficult questions. Some still are searching, and some questions are still difficult.

---

[18] Written by: Bob Dylan. Released: August 1963. Recorded: Peter, Paul and Mary.

"LIKE A ROLLING STONE"

"Therefore, let him who thinks he stands take heed lest he fall." 1 Corinthians 10: 12

Bob Dylan was certainly a storyteller and an observer of human nature. He starts this song in classic story-telling fashion, "Once upon a time you..." And thus, begins one of his most definitive hit songs which not only he recorded but numerous others did also.

It tells a classic story of someone who had it all at one time: fine clothes, money to spend, friends, parties, education and lost it all. The advice of well-meaning friends who warned this person to be careful you are headed for a fall, went unheeded. To me, it is the story of a prodigal. It is also the story told by one who seems to relish in the fall of one they envy.

The song repeatedly asks questions of this person: how does it feel now, to be by yourself, disconnected and left on their own? To have lost it all and now are without directions or a way home is the recurrent theme. How does it feel to be like the proverbial rolling stone? If you have been a prodigal or love a prodigal, you know this cycle well. I heard a story of a group of writers who were gathered together and talking about writing. Ernest Hemingway was there, as the story goes and claimed he could write a short story in less than 10 words. As it turns out he only used six: "For Sale: Baby Shoes, never worn." Now whether that story is true or not, it certainly brings a picture to mind of a young woman with a sad countenance as she looks at the baby shoes still wrapped in the box by an empty cradle in the corner. Dylan's song paints the same picture of a life's ups and downs and the consequences of wrong decisions. There are sad stories all about us. Empty lives like the empty cradle. Thoughts which keep one awake long into the night of, "What could have been, if only I had_____." You probably have a decision you wished you had not made. But God can restore and fill that empty space.

There is a story within this song, a short-story which lasted a little over six minutes. But the depth of despair is found in the repeated lament of a lost person with no direction home. Do you see the prodigal standing in the pig pen? Do you see the once pretty princess Dylan has described, down and out and humbled? With her head bowed in shame and so tired of this life and filled with regrets. Maybe you passed her today with her handwritten sign—"Hungry, Homeless and Helpless. Please Help. God Bless." You wanted to tell yourself it was a sham, a professional beggar, or someone who wasted their opportunities. Do you personally know how it feels to be on your own? To be lost without direction in your life. To not know a single soul. Like the proverbial rolling stone which gathers no moss. Unrooted and unloved.

There is a Father waiting for his son or daughter to come to their senses. Repentance is coming to your senses, a change of mind which leads to a change of direction. Maybe what they need is for you to stop and ask them, "Are you on your own? Do you need directions home?

"Like A Rolling Stone"[19]

Bob Dylan was a writer. He wrote songs, poems and prose. This song came out of 20 pages of his extended writing which reflected his introspective thinking. This certainly was not a love ballad. He distilled the lengthy writing into a six minute 13 second recording. Released as a single, it was on both sides. To play the entire song, the disc jockey had to flip the record over.

The song began as a folk ballad but was changed during the recording session and finally ended up in a rock and roll format. This was a complete change from the acoustic, folk-singing Bob Dylan. It was rock and roll. To me it was a story as old as the Prodigal Son, but this time a prodigal daughter, a princess who had it all and lost it.

Was the perspective of the writer one of revenge? Was it about someone Dylan knew? As a

---

[19] Composer and singer: Bob Dylan. Released on Columbia Records: June 1965. Reached: No.2 on Billboard; No. 1 on Cashbox . Included in album: Highway 61 Revisited. Selected by the magazine, Rolling Stone as the Number 1 song of their list of the 500 Greatest Hits.

result, lyrics were discussed for endless hours. It could not be reduced to: "I gave it a 90, it had a good beat and was easy to dance to"

This was a poet who found just the right style of music to put his words to and Bob Dylan was transformed from folk music star to rock and roll superstar and a poet for sure.

The song was cruel in some ways as the listener hears the envy and jealousy in the lyrics over this woman's seemingly perfect life. The lyrics turn into glee when the one who had everything, fell and lost it all. Like Ella Fitzgerald's hit song of another generation: "Goody, Goody," it sounds like a song of a jilted lover who is celebrating her former lover getting his heart broken. Perhaps this person blessed with looks, money and popularity treated this person with indifference or even ridiculed them. Now they have fallen on hard times and you hear the jeering voice: "How does it feel now, Miss High and Mighty?" Jesus said I will never leave you nor forsake you. I have called you friend. Down on your luck? Need a friend? Need direction? Call Jesus, He knows the way home. He is closer than you think.

"ONE FOR THE MONEY, TWO FOR THE SHOW, THREE TO GET READY"

"I go now to prepare a place for you, so that where I am you will be also." John 14;

The popular phrase in the title is recognized as the kick-off of the classic Rock-a-Billy hit by Carl Perkins' "Blue Suede Shoes." Where did this phrase originate? It is a Mother Goose rhyme: "One to make ready, two to prepare, good luck to the rider and away goes the mare." This, obviously, was a race-starting rhyme. This became the popular, 'one for the money, two for the show, three to get ready and four to go! Seems this is still the start of another race, the human race, or as we often cynically call it—the "rat race."

One for the money: Ask most people what they would ask for if they could get anything they wanted, and most will ask for a large sum of money. Why? Because they equate money with happiness or the ability to have all your needs met and the freedom to live a worry-free life. **Two** for the show: This money would buy them a lavish home, or homes, travel, best clothes, jewelry, cars, etc. If you got it, flaunt it type of lifestyle. The lifestyle of the rich and famous. **Three** to Get Ready: Get ready for what? Can one play golf every day? Spend every day at the beach? Go shopping for endless hours and eat out every meal? Guess what these activities would become? BORING! And what about your friends? Are they your friends or want what you can buy for them and the places you can take them?

Four says 'away we go.' Where are you going? What lies ahead? Jesus tells us heaven is a prepared place for prepared people. How does one prepare? What must I do to be saved? This is the very question the Philippian jailer ask Paul and Silas. And Paul told the jailer: "Believe on the Lord Jesus Christ and you will be saved, and your household."(Acts 16)

Carl Perkins was one of the most influential pioneers in a genre called, "rock-a-billy."He was also one of the most down-to-earth people I have ever met. He often came into my in-law's music store to buy Ernie Ball strings where I worked for a brief time. The first time he came into the store, I called him, Mr. Perkins. He smiled, stuck out his hand and said, "Call me Carl." One day, I had been pulling out some old sheet music and found some copies of the sheet music to "Blue Suede Shoes." The next time Carl came in, I showed him the sheet music. He laughed when he saw it and said he had never seen the sheet music before. He pointed to the sport coat he was wearing in the photograph and said, "I had to borrow that sport coat, because I did not have one." A man who had become a legend, but remained a humble man. That is how I remember Carl Perkins.

"Blue Suede Shoes"[20]

Carl Perkins grew up in a poor farming family. He grew up around the Gospel music sung in his church and in the cotton fields by Afro Americans with whom Carl picked cotton. He loved the Grand Ole Opry and listened to it faithfully on his father's radio. He loved music. His first guitar was a homemade guitar of a cigar box, a broomstick and strings.

"Blue Suede Shoes" would be Perkins' only number 1 hit as a performer. This song would be covered by many artists, including another young upcoming star named Elvis Presley. The flip side of "Blue Suede Shoes was "Honey Don't"later covered by the Beatles, admirers of Perkins' music and writing. It is considered a classic rock and roll song and a new genre called, 'rockabilly."

Perkins and his brother Jay were on their way to stardom. After performing in Norfolk, Va. on March 21, 1956, they were headed for New York City to appear on the Perry Como Show. A wreck would postpone Perkins' appearance. His brother Jay fractured his neck and suffered severe internal injuries from which he never fully recovered.

---

[20] Composed by Carl Perkins . Recorded by Carl Perkins on Sun Record label. Released: January, 1956. Charts: No.1 Billboard Country Music Chart; No. 2 on Billboard Best Sellers Pop Music and No. 3 on the Rhythm and Blues Chart.

Drummer W.S. Holland saved Carl who had landed face down, unconscious in a ditch of water.

Perkins continued to tour, perform and write. In 1964 he was convinced to tour England with Chuck Berry. He played to large crowds and ended up one night at party with the Beatles who were fans of Carl Perkins. Paul McCartney later said, "if there hadn't been a Carl Perkins, there would have never been the Beatles."

In 1968, Carl Perkins tells the story of how he was touring with Johnny Cash and went on a four-day drinking binge. With their tour bus parked on the beach, Carl Perkins fell on his knees and took the bottle of whiskey and threw into the ocean. Perkins said he prayed this prayer: "Lord, I'm going to throw this bottle away. I'm going to show You I believe in You. I sailed it into the Pacific and got up, knowing I had done the right thing," Perkins and Cash helped each other stay sober. One for the money—Blue Suede Shoes provided Carl and his family much needed *money*; Two for th Show—I'm going to *show* you Lord I believe in you. Three to get *ready* to live his life for the Lord, his family and community. Four to *go*-Carl Perkins passed away on January 19, 1998. At his funeral, George Harrison sang "My Sweet Lord." Carl was a great musician, an even better human being, and his work to help abused children is still going on in Jackson, Tennessee, Home of the Extraordinary Carl Perkins.

"NOTHING FROM NOTHING (LEAVES NOTHING)"

"In the beginning God created the heavens and the earth. And the earth was without form and void; and darkness was on the face of the deep. And the Spirit of God was hovering over the face of the waters." Genesis 1: 1&2

The Hebrew word for created is "bara." It means to bring something out of nothing. Man is very clever at making something out of something, but only God can create something out of nothing. The question we all must answer for ourselves is how did all this (creation, the earth, the universe) get here? Everything must be created twice. Once in the mind of the creator who had the end in mind before the beginning. And the second time when the creator creates that which he has seen in his mind. First, the idea, the concept which produces a plan, a design or blueprint to create the creation step-by-step. This means the design has a purpose and intent. Now the alternative belief is in the beginning there was matter which existed. How did this matter come to be? For what purpose or intent? This matter then evolved in to higher, more complex forms until finally—human beings were formed. Really? How? For what purpose?

I recently heard Vince Vitali from the Ravi Zacharias Institute speak and he said, "We all have to believe something extraordinary." What we believe about creation impacts our world view. The Book of

Genesis is the foundation for the rest of the Bible. This story, God's story gives our lives meaning and purpose. It tells us where we came from, our purpose which gives our lives meaning. It defines good and evil for us. It gives our lives value and significance. God is the author of this story and the author of life. He tells us our destiny. Is life "a tale told by an idiot full of sound and fury, signifying nothing" as Macbeth opined? Or is there a larger story we are part of which gives meaning to our lives? I have discovered life without God is meaningless.

The Biblical Worldview starts with God, while the atheist worldview starts with the universe. In the 20th century the Big Bang theory came to be accepted, which said the universe did not always exist but came into being with an explosion of great magnitude, thus the name, "Big Bang." If there is a big bang, there must be a Big Banger. We are told all things were created by Him and for Him. The atheist asked who created your God? Our God is uncreated, pre-existent. He created everything. If you believe your creator is the universe, who created the universe? Even science admits the earth benefits from everything being just right to support life. They call it the "Goldilocks Effect."

Here is what we know about God from creation. He is Sovereign, everything is under His control. The earth spins on its axis and revolves around the sun at just the right distance. He is Holy, that is pure and good. From His goodness all good and evil are defined. He possesses all knowledge. And He is Immutable, un-changing. Besides all this—nothing from nothing leaves nothing and only God can make something from nothing. I find this makes more sense than any other theory. An extraordinary God who does the extraordinary every day!

"Nothing from Nothing"[21]

Billy Preston was a child prodigy. Watch him perform this hit song on American Bandstand, his fingers flying effortlessly over the keyboard. Entirely self-taught. Never had a music lesson, yet by age 10 he was playing organ for Gospel Great, Mahalia Jackson.

He stayed busy during the 1960s in the studio as a top session keyboardist. He was in recording sessions for: Little Richard, Sam Cooke, Ray Charles, Gospel singer James Cleveland.

He also was used by Eric Clapton and the Rolling Stones.

The Beatles called him the "Fifth Beatle," and gave him credit on one of their records.

Guess what the flip side of his number one hit, "Nothing from Nothing" was? Here is a hint, Billy wrote this for his mother, but it was Joe Cocker's

---

[21] Written by Billy Preston & Bruce Fisher. Recorded by Billy Preston. Released: 1974. Charts: No. 1 on Billboard Hot 100; No.1 on Cash Box Top Hits.

rendition which became famous. The flip-side was : "You Are So Beautiful."

Billy Preston later said he was sexually abused as a child. It created confusion and trouble for the young boy and drugs and bad decisions led him down the wrong path. He would die at age 59. Billy Preston loved making music. You can see the joy in him when he performs. For him it all began in church worshipping a Creator God.

"IMAGINE"

"Eye has not seen, nor ear heard, nor have entered into the heart of man the things which God has prepared for those who love Him." 1 Corinthians 2:9. God is saying you cannot imagine what wonderful things I have prepared for you. And we are told: "Now to Him who is able to do exceedingly, abundantly above all that we ask or think…"implies we cannot in our wildest imaginations imagine the wonderful blessings which await us. Ephesians 3: 20.

Imagination is a gift of God that only we humans have. God speaks to our imagination in the Bible. Now as we think of John Lennon's song, "Imagine," we know he uses his imagination to imagine a world without heaven or hell. Interestingly a popular Christian Gospel song and movie is entitled: "I Can Only Imagine" speaks of the wonder of heaven and imagining seeing the Lord face to face. So, imagination can be used for good or evil. There are two potters who wish to shape our thinking. God wants to shape our thoughts for He knows as a man thinks in his heart, so is he. The devil wants to conform our thinking to accept the world's view. Therefore, we are told to be not conformed by the world but be transformed by the Word of God. Ads bombard us daily as to what will fulfill our longings. Every week people spend hundreds of millions of dollars for lottery tickets, imagining what all they can do with such a windfall. Let me ask you a question, dear reader: Can you imagine a God who knows you intimately and loves you beyond anything you can imagine? "He (God) who did not spare His own Son, but delivered Him up for us all, how shall He not with Him also freely give us all things?" Romans 8:32. (One of my favorite verses)

A.W. Tozer said: "What comes to our minds when we think about God is the most important thing about us." Paul writes: "That you should no longer walk as the rest of the Gentiles walk, in the futility of their minds, having their understanding darkened, being alienated from the life of God, because of the ignorance that is in them, because of the blindness of their hearts. Who, being past feeling have given themselves over to lewdness, to work all uncleanness with greediness?" Ephesians 4: 17-19. These verses describe imagination gone bad. Just like in the days of Noah, the thoughts of their hearts were on evil all the time.

What if, as a believer, everything in your life was a part of God's wise plan? What would this do to your worrying and anxiety if you believed He was working it all together for good. God's wisdom means God will bring about the best possible results, by the best possible means, for the most possible people, for the longest period of time. If there was a better way, God would use it. If there was a faster, easier way to get the best results He would have chosen it. God withholds no good thing from those who walk uprightly. "God has promised good to me, His Word my hope secures. My shield and portion He will be as long as life endures." Amazing Grace. Imagine that!

"Imagine"[22]

This was the most successful and popular song of Lennon's solo career after leaving the Beatles. In 2012, this song and album was voted 80th on the Rolling Stone Magazine's list of 500 Greatest Albums.

John asked former Beatle, George Harrison, to perform on this album. The album was first begun at Ascot Sound Studios and finished at the Record Plant in New York City with Phil Specter joining Lennon and Yoko Ono as co-producer on "Imagine."

Lennon later said Yoko should have been credited as co-writer as he was inspired by her poetry.

Lennon said his motivation for the song was world peace. After Lennon's death, the song rose on the charts again.

As a side note, Lennon and McCartney had a rather bitter break up of their partnership. McCartney went to court to dissolve the partnership. Lennon wrote and recorded a song entitled, "How Do You Sleep?" This album was written in retaliation against McCartney's alleged attacks on Lennon and Ono.

---

[22] Written by: John Lennon. Recorded by: John Lennon. Released: October 1971 . Charts: No 1 in US, the UK, Australia, Japan, Germany.

PEOPLE GET READY

We were all sad when the Beatles broke up. And I cried the day John Lennon died. But now I cannot imagine the Beatles having continued as the Rolling Stones have. They remain forever young in our minds as those four British lads who I first saw on a February Sunday night in my college dorm in 1964, 55 years ago. There are so many memories we associate with their songs. The power of music.

"WHAT'S YOUR NAME?"

"Therefore God also has highly exalted Him and given Him a name which is above every name, that at the name of Jesus every knee shall bow, of those in heaven, and those on earth, and of those under the earth, and that every tongue should confess that Jesus Christ is Lord, to the glory of God the Father." Philippians 2: 9-11

In this song, the writer asks the first question we usually ask when we meet someone for the first time: "What's your name?" Men usually then ask other men what they do, for men often define themselves by their work. Peter referred to Simon as Simon the Tanner, for example. In the Bible names had significance. They carried meaning and perhaps expressed the desires of the parents of what they wanted this new child to grow up and become. One notices also in the Bible there was only one name given and often someone would be associated or differentiated by denoting who their father was, as in David, son of Jesse. Sometimes a description would be added to describe a person. There were several people named James in the New Testament. One of the disciples about whom we know very little was named James, the Lesser. Perhaps this meant he was younger than James the brother of John, the sons of Zebedee. Surnames did not appear and become popular until around 1100 A.D.

Joseph and Mary were told by the angels, "And you shall call His name Jesus; for He shall save His people from their sins." As the verse above tells us this name was above all other names. Why is this name so supreme and so powerful? We are told of the power of this name. Peter said in Acts 4: 12: "Nor is there salvation in any other, for there is no other name under heaven given among men by which we must be saved."

Jesus said if we ask anything in His Name, I will do it. (John 14: 14). The Bible also tells us this name has the power to supply our needs. Philippians 4: 19 says, "But my God shall supply all of your needs according to His riches in glory by Christ Jesus."

Jesus is the name of our Advocate with the Father. If we sin, He is our Advocate, our lawyer who pleads our innocence. Jesus is the name of the Carpenter who wiped out the handwriting of requirements against us, which was contrary to us. And He has taken it out of the way, having nailed it to the cross. (Colossians 2:14).

Jesus is the name of the Carpenter of Nazareth who constructed a bridge to heaven with a handful of nails and an old rugged cross. Jesus is the name of my High Priest, My Redeemer who paid for my sin. Jesus is the Cornerstone, the Rock on whom I have built my life. His name means all of this and more. Jesus is the name of the author of life and the author of the Bible. There is something about that name! The writer of this song, "What's Your Name," speaks of waiting his whole life for this person to come along. Jesus is waiting for you at the corner of the crossroads of the Broad Way and the Narrow Way.

He already knows your name and wants to record it in the Lamb's Book of Life.

"What's Your Name?"[23]

This song written by Juan Johnson was considered a classic "doo-wop" genre. Johnson had previously been a part of the 'doo-wop' group, "The Genies."

Ronald 'Don' Trone and Claude "Juan" Johnson were a R&B duo out of Long Beach, N.Y.

They were another of those "one-hit wonders" who never scored another top hit. They continued to play the clubs and tour with other groups. Like many 'one-hit wonders' little is known about them before and after. But anyone coming of age when this song was popular can immediately began to sing along when we hear it being played.

Trone would pass away in 1982 at age 45. Johnson would continue to perform with different partners. Johnson died in 2002 at age 67.

This song was nominated recently to the Doo Wop Hall of Fame.

---

[23] Written by Claude "Juan" Johnson. Recorded by: Don & Juan. Release Date: 1962. Charts: No. 7 on Billboard Pop Chart.

"Do You Want to Know a Secret?"

"The *secret things* belong to the Lord our God, but those things which are revealed belong to us and to our children forever, that we may do all the words of His law." Deuteronomy 29:29.

In this song, another hit song by the Beatles, the requirement for knowing the secret is you must promise not to tell. The secret I want to share with you is one I have promised to tell and share with everyone. It is THE SECRET OF LIVING. Jesus said He came to share the secret of living with us. The problem is we have an enemy who does not want us to hear the secret. He is called a thief (the devil, Satan, our adversary) and he wants to kill, and steal and destroy. Jesus said He came that we might have life and have it more abundantly. John 10:10

How tragic to go through life and not discover the purpose of life, the secret of living. If you do not discover this secret, you can end up wasting your most valuable possession—your very life. We must understand who we are, which explains why we are here. Ready for this information? I pray you will seriously consider what Jesus taught his disciples and us just hours before He knew He was to die. It is found in John 15. Here are the important elements in this metaphor: "I am the Vine, and My Father is the vinedresser."(Implied also is the Holy Spirit, the life-giving sap which the branch receives by being attached.) A vine in a vineyard. The owner of the vineyard, the Constant Gardener and Vinedresser. The attached branch. The fruit produced.

1. The secret of life is fruit bearing. God said to Adam and Eve, "Be fruitful and multiply." You were created to be a fruit-bearing branch. Jesus is the vine. You become a branch in the Vine by placing your faith in Jesus Christ to save your life from its emptiness, thus giving your life meaning and purpose.

2. The secret of fruit bearing is abiding. A branch apart from the Vine can do nothing. The Holy Spirit within us, provides the life-giving, life-transforming, life-sustaining "sap" which produces the fruit which the branch bears.

3. The secret of abiding is obeying. If one wishes to enjoy good health, they must obey the laws of good health: proper nutrition, exercise, no harmful habits, smoking, etc. This is true of the laws of abiding, to disobey the laws of the vine and the branch is to separate yourself from the blessings of obedience and you cannot bear fruit on your own.

4. The secret of obeying is loving. Jesus said if you love me, you will keep my commandments. A new mother does not care for her newborn child because of the laws of the land can take away a child from a mother who is unfit and does not care for her child. She does it because she loves this child. Love is always the highest motivation for obedience. Love, not the fear of punishment makes obeying easiest.

5. The secret of loving is knowing. Jesus said, "This is life eternal, to know the true and living God and the One Whom He has sent.' John 17:3. Warren Wiersbe, has a great little book, "5 Secrets of Living" by Tyndale Publishers. I strongly recommend it for your reading. Now you know the secret.

"Do You Want to Know a Secret?"[24]

This was one of the few songs on which lead guitarist, George Harrison was selected as lead vocalist.

Lennon said, "George was not the greatest singer in the world. He only had three notes. But he has greatly improved." Harrison would later record a number one hit with a romantic ballad entitled: "Something."

Lennon says the song was inspired by the tune, "I'm Wishing," from the Walt Disney animated film, "Snow White and the Seven Dwarfs."

Interesting side note, since this was inspired by an animated cartoon character, Alvin and the Chipmunks covered the song in an album released in 1964, "The Chipmunks Sing the Beatles."

---

[24] Written by: John Lennon/Paul McCartney. Released: March 1964. Recorded by: The Beatles. Charts: Reached #2 behind "Can't Buy Me Love"by the Beatles.

PEOPLE GET READY

The song was written in 1962. It was part of a marathon recording session in 1963 to fill an album entitled "Please, Please Me!" It was later released as a single. From an inspiration of a 1937 song in an animated film to its final stage in a song featuring George Harrison in his first lead vocals, now you know the secret of a song's journey.

How about you and your journey? Do you know the secret of what and who you are, why you are here, and where you came from? The Lord wants you to know the secret and I have promised to tell you.

"BRIDGE OVER TROUBLED WATER"

"And besides all this, between us and you there is a great gulf fixed, so that those want to pass from here to you cannot, nor can those from there pass to us." Luke 16: 26.

Bridges are very important. They allow one to cross over obstacles or impasses which they would not otherwise be able to cross. A bridge is a span over those impassable areas which connect two things together. It must be strong enough to bear the load.

In this parable told by the Lord Jesus in Luke 16, two men have died. The rich man has ended up in a place of torment, and Lazarus the beggar has ended up in a place of peace and comfort. The rich man in torment wants someone to come over and supply him with water for he is thirsty, but there is not a bridge over this troubled water in this place. One can sense the audience riveted to every word of this story. The man in the place of torment then requests Abraham, to whom he is talking, send this man in the place of comfort on the other side to go warn his five brothers about this place so they will not end up in this place of torment. Father Abraham tells the man, they have the Bible to tell them what they need to do. The man says they need to hear from someone raised from the dead or they will not repent. Abraham says, if they will not believe Moses and the prophets, they will not believe someone who has risen from the dead. (Luke 16: 19-31) I urge you to read this story. Why? Because this bridge over troubled water can only be passed over in this life, not the next.

Jesus was a carpenter. It is not by accident Jesus' occupation was that of a carpenter. For He came to lay a foundation. I believe one of the things Jesus would have been known for building in his carpenter shop in Nazareth was smooth yokes which rested easy on the shoulders. Yokes are designed to distribute the weight and make load carrying easier. Therefore, in Matthew 11, Jesus says "Come to Me, all you who labor and are heavy laden, and I will give you rest. Take My yoke upon you and learn from Me, for I am gentle and lowly in heart and you will find rest for your souls. My yoke is easy, and My burden is light."(Matthew 11:28-30)

Jesus the Carpenter of Nazareth and Son of God has built a bridge to span that fixed gulf between sinful man and Holy God. He built it with an old rugged cross and a handful of nails. Do not wait too late to cross this bridge. This bridge can only be crossed in this life. Dante in his classic, "Inferno" passes through the gate of Hell which bears an inscription with Dante's famous quote: "Abandon all hope, ye who enter here." God is the God of all hope. Jesus said, "God so loved the world He gave His only begotten son, that whosoever should believe in Him should not perish but have everlasting life." John 3: 16.

"Bridge Over Troubled Waters"[25]

An unusual pair, Paul Simon and Art Garfunkel were part of an off shoot of folk music and rock known as folk rock. When you would see their names, they would be described as the 'folk-rock duo.'

Paul Simon was the writer and composer. Garfunkel was drawn to acting and won a Golden Globe for his skills. Simon was the musician, always learning, always exploring and experimenting. Their work followed an unusual schedule and style. Garfunkel might take an acting role and Simon would then retreat to write for 3 or 4 months. Then they would both go into the studio for 3-4 months to record.

"Scarborough Fair," "Homeward Bound," "Parsley, Sage & Rosemary Thyme" bring to mind their harmonies.

And who can forget the music track to "The Graduate," starring Dustin Hoffman in the Mike Nichols classic movie of the '60s. The track laid down by Simon and Garfunkel was amazing as it also followed the story line. Who can ever forget Anne Bancroft as, "Mrs. Robinson?"

---

[25] Written by Paul Simon. Recorded by Simon and Garfunkel. Released: January 1970. Charts: No, 1 on Billboard Top 100 Hits. The album by the same name was named album of the year and song of the year by Grammy Awards for that year.

This song, "Bridge Over Troubled Waters," was influenced by Simon's interest in gospel music. This song had the feel and tone, sound and wording of Gospel music.

It was done as a solo, featuring Art Garfunkel. Simon insisted Art was to be the one to sing this song. 1970 would be their biggest year and their last year. They did come together again for a concert in Central Park, and Simon went on with a solo career and other hits.

The "sail on silver girl" lyric in the song was a reference to Paul's wife, Peggy, who had recently developed a few silver threads of hair.

Bridges take us places we cannot reach on our own. Bridges connect us. Have you found the Bridge over Troubled Waters the Lord Jesus has built for you?

"TEMPTED BY THE FRUIT OF ANOTHER"

"And the Lord God commanded the man saying, "Of every tree in the Garden you may freely eat; but of the tree of the knowledge of good and evil you shall not eat, for in the day that you eat of it you shall surely die." (Genesis 2: 16, 17)

"Let no one say when he is tempted, I am tempted by God"; for God cannot be tempted by evil, nor does He Himself tempt anyone. But each one is tempted when he is drawn away by his own desires and enticed. Then, when desire has conceived, it gives birth to sin; and sin, when it is full-grown, brings forth death." (James 1: 13-15)

There were two trees in the Garden: The Tree of Life and the Tree of the Knowledge of Good and Evil. Our family tree traces its roots back to the Tree of the Knowledge of Good and Evil, for when Adam and Eve ate of the tree in the garden, we inherited their sinful natures. This is because each creature and creation reproduced after their own kind. Therefore, we have to be born again, according to the Lord Jesus as He told Nicodemus in John 3.

Genesis 3 tells us about the temptation, and we can see this method of creating doubt in God's Word is still the strategy today. The temptation rests on three areas: lust of the flesh, lust of the eyes and the pride of life. The temptation to eat the fruit of another tree is the playbook by which the enemy still operates.

This temptation was the first advertising campaign. Notice the first step is to make you disappointed with what you have by creating doubt that you have everything that would satisfy your desires. The plot then involves reducing the risk associated with giving into this temptation: "You will not surely die." Once the risk is reduced, the interest increases proportionally. This brings the deception of a greater enjoyment which comes from eating this fruit. You will not only NOT die; you will be wise like God. Then the woman saw it was good for food, and pleasant to the eyes and would make one wise, she took and ate and gave to her husband also. Their perfect bodies, the earthen vessels were marred. Guilt and shame entered immediately. When God came for His daily visit with His creation, they hid from God. Sin produces guilt, fear, and shame, and makes one want to hide their sin. Notice something very important—God came seeking them and made a cover for their nakedness. Christianity is the only religion where God comes looking for man, all others are the story of man looking for God.

Our problem is two-fold: our inherited old sinful nature and our sins. Our sin nature must be dealt with and our sins must be paid for. Calvary accomplished both. Our old nature was crucified with Jesus and His blood paid for our sins, all of them and yours too, dear reader. How then do we resist sin? "Thy Word have I hid in my heart, that I might not sin against you." (Psalm 119: 11). You now have weapons and armor which are mighty and able to transform your mind to keep you from yielding to temptation. Learn what to do when tempted by the fruit of another.

"Tempted by the Fruit of Another"[26]

Squeeze is a British group which like a lot of groups had changes over the years. This song comes from their East Side Story album.

Although it only broke barely into the Top 40 in the US market it became popular due to its use in commercials: Burger King and Heineken Beer.

It has elements of rock, plus a sound called, "blue-eyed soul," as well as a genre identified as new wave.

Elvis Costello, who produced it can be heard in the backup vocals. The song was inspired and came to the writers as they were in a taxi headed for Heathrow Airport to begin a tour. Thus, the opening line, 'I bought a toothbrush.' At their concerts many bring toothbrushes and throw them on the stage.

The story hints at a bit of nostalgia as they recall memories as they pass certain locations. There seems to have been a relationship which has failed or is failing, perhaps including unfaithfulness.

It is one of those songs left for the hearer to interpret what's going on—but an interesting story.

---

[26] Written by: Difford & Tilbrook. Recorded by: Squeeze. Released: 1981. Charts: Top 40 in USA. Produced by Elvis Costello.

One which draws one in with a beat which makes your feet pat and want to dance.

Sting, Joe Cocker, Rita Coolidge are a few who have also recorded this song.

The tag line is as old as the Garden of Eden. Tempted, seduced and then the truth is discovered too late. The Tempter is a deceiver. Sin will take you further than you wanted to go; keep you longer than you wanted to stay and cost you more than you wanted to pay. Have you discovered this truth?

"HOW CAN I BE SURE?"

"Inasmuch as many have taken in hand to set in order a narrative of those things which have been fulfilled among us, just as those who from the beginning were eyewitnesses and ministers of the word delivered to us, it seemed good to me also, having had perfect understanding of all things from the very first, to write to you an orderly account, most excellent Theophilus, that *you may know with certainty of those things in which I have instructed you."* Luke 1: 1-4.

Thus begins Dr. Luke's gospel which was written to make sure the reader can trust the story of Jesus. Dr. Luke, who traveled with the apostle Paul, was a Greek physician and a first-rate historian. Thomas Arnold, Professor of History at Oxford, and author of the three volume History of Rome stated: "I know of no fact in the history of mankind which is proved by better and fuller evidence of every sort, to the understanding of a fair enquirer, than the great sign which God has given us that Christ died and rose again from the dead."

The Bible says we are to examine ourselves to see if we are in the faith. We are to test ourselves.

Here is the simple question to ask to test yourself: "Do you know Jesus?" Do you have a real relationship with Him? The foundation for any relationship is communication. Communicating with Jesus consists of only two things:

1. Talking to Him (Prayer)

2. Hearing from Him. (Speaks to you through His word)

Let's take the first one, talking to Jesus. When was the last time you prayed to Him? Prayer is a critical part of our relationship. Plus, Jesus wants to hear from you. He encourages you to call on Him.

Hearing from Jesus. This is where some people think we are crazy if we say Jesus talks to us. He talks to us through His Word. If you are not personalizing scripture which was written for us, you are missing a blessing. For example: In Luke 23: 34 put your name in this verse: "Then Jesus said, "Father forgive _____ (Your name) for he/she does not know what they do." His words also transform our minds by replacing thoughts which were wrong with ones with are right. These are two basics which should reveal a real relationship.

But remember 'whosoever calls upon the name of the Lord shall be saved."(Romans 10:13) Have you called upon the name of Jesus? He is waiting for you. Call Him. I promise you He wants you to call Him. He knows your heart and its longings. He knows the burdens He wants to help you bear. It will be the most important call you ever make. How can I be sure? Because I made that call on September 16, 1977 as a 31-year-old alcoholic at the point of suicide. I prayed "Lord Jesus if you are real, come into my life and save me." He is real. I am saved, sober and sane. An honest doubter who was given assurance.

"How Can I Be Sure?"[27]

In 1965, Felix started a group called, "The Young Rascals." In 1966, they had their first hit, "Good Loving' which rose to No. 1. What followed was a phenomenal outburst of great songs.

"Good Loving" was followed up with "Grooving "in 1967 and from the album of Grooving comes this hit song, "How Can I Be Sure?"

Cavaliere says the inspiration for this song came from a young lady he was dating at the time. He was confused about their relationship and their age difference.

He also said he was influenced by the Beatles who had the courage to change to slower ballads with "Michele "and "Yesterday."

Other hits those of us from this time will remember are: "A Beautiful Morning" and "Got To Be Free."

The group broke up, but their string of hits earned the membership in the Rock and Roll Hall of Fame. In addition, Felix Cavaliere was inducted into the Writers Hall of Fame.

Felix keeps a busy schedule touring at age 76.

---

[27] Written by Felix Cavaliere and Eddie Briganti. Recorded by: Young Rascals . Released: 1967. Charts: No. 4 on the Billboard Top 100. Their 4th top 10 Hit in a row. Felix Cavaliere was a member of Joey Dee and the Starlighters who had a hit with the "Peppermint Twist."

"I'M A BELIEVER, (NOT A DOUBT IN MY MIND)"

"These things I have written to you who believe in the name of the Son of God, that you may know that you have eternal life and that you may continue to believe in the name of the Son of God." I John 5: 13.

Doubt is defined as: "to be uncertain about something; to believe something may not be true or is unlikely; to have no confidence in." Everyone must deal with doubt, be it Christians or non-Christians, the intellectual skeptic or the born-again believer. The Virgin Mary had doubts when an angel told her she would be with child and she doubted saying 'how can this be?' Sarah laughed to herself when she overheard the Pre-incarnate Lord tell Abraham she would have a son by this time next year. Both women were doubtful because of their condition or status. Sarah was old and past child-bearing age and had always been barren. Mary was a virgin and unmarried. The man in Mark 9 with the son who had seizures and could not find a cure was doubtful, because his previous experience told him no one could help his son.

Doubt is the enemy of faith. It was first used in Genesis 3 when the devil casts doubt on God's Word. He is still using the same method. The scientists scoff at the notion of immaculate conception. "Impossible" he says, "physically and scientifically." This same scientist might believe we came from the universe. How can this be? Who created the universe? No one. Then they must believe it created itself. Does that not sound impossible? Yet they believe this.

I love the story told in Matthew 14 when Jesus walked on the water to the disciples in their boat. They were fearful and thought it must be a ghost. For it is impossible to walk on water. Jesus called out to them and said, "Take courage. It is I. Fear not." Peter wanted assurance and said, "If it is you Lord bid me to come to you." Jesus issued a one word enabling command: "Come." Peter stepped out and walked on the water. But he saw the wind and began to sink and cried out to the Lord to save him, and the Lord did. Then the Lord Jesus said, "Oh you of little faith, why did you doubt?" Why do we doubt His word? The enemy takes our eyes off him with waves of trouble. We waver. We doubt. James says when we ask, we must believe and not doubt, because James writes, "Let not that man who doubts suppose he will receive anything." "He is like a wave of the sea driven and tossed by the wind. That man is double-minded and unstable in all his ways." (James 1).

There are two types of doubters: an honest doubter, who wants to know the truth; and a dishonest doubter who looks for ways not to believe. Here is the prayer of an honest doubter, the father of the boy possessed by a spirit that has robbed him of speech. When Jesus told him, nothing was impossible to those who believe. The man prayed: "Lord, I believe. Help my unbelief." (Mark 9 :24). The prayer of a man desperate to believe, an honest doubter who wanted to believe the truth. His son was healed. He walked away without a doubt in his mind.

"I'm A Believer, (Not a Doubt in My Mind) [28]

The Monkees were an example of art imitating life. A comedy show which featured 4 young musicians who are trying to break into the music business. Their similarity to the Beatles was obvious, including a British musician. Each week featured a comedic episode but always the music. The show ran from the fall of 1966 until January of 1968.

This song, "I'm A Believer" written by Neil Diamond was released in November of 1966. The Monkees performed the song on their weekly TV show, and it went to number 1 by the end of December 1966.

It remained at number 1 for seven weeks, becoming the biggest-selling record for all of 1967. Billboard ranked the song, number 5 for the entire year. This record went gold in two days.

It would go on to sell over 10 million copies! Fewer than 40 single records have achieved this volume. This is the power of media to influence and

---

[28] Written by Neil Diamond. Recorded by: The Monkees. Released: November 1966. Charts: No. 1 Billboard.

sell us its ideas. Jesus did not rely on media, there was none. Yet His message is called 'good news.' This record by the Monkees sold 10 million copies fifty years ago.

Did you know the Bible sold 3.9 billion copies over the last 50 years? The bestselling book written during the last 50 years was "Harry Potter," which sold a paltry 400 million copies.

Have you read the Best Seller? Read it and I believe you can know for sure.

"YOU'VE GOT A FRIEND"

"Greater love has no one than this, than to lay down one's life for his friends." (John 15: 13)

Jesus spoke these words on the night of his arrest. He would soon be going to the cross to lay down His life for us. What a friend we have in Jesus!

In this popular song one of the lines which is repeated is all you have to do is call my name and I will come running. In my mind I see the father of the prodigal in Luke 15 running while the son was still a great way off. See him lifting his robe in order not to trip. This older man with two grown sons running with reckless abandon to greet his long lost son. Joy overcomes him so; he cannot stop kissing the prodigal son who is trying to get out his confession he has rehearsed all the way home. The father makes plans for a feast, a party of celebration. Jesus tells us this is nothing compared to the rejoicing in heaven when one sinner repents. Can you imagine the scene in heaven the day you repented of your sins? The cheering and applause in heaven were louder than any football game you have ever attended. Tears of joy ran down this father's cheeks in this story. Those tears are what my momma called a 'good cry.'

The audience which heard this story recorded in Luke 15 some 2000 years ago was typical of the crowds who gathered to hear Jesus. We are told there were great multitudes following this man called Jesus. In the crowds were a variety of different people, a cross section of the culture. The crowds consisted of tax collectors, sinners, prostitutes, drunkards, and the Pharisees and Scribes. (This story had something for everyone) There was unconditional love for the prodigals, and the sinners, and for the Pharisees and Scribes—an unflattering picture of themselves in the self-righteous elder brother. Jesus wanted all of them to repent and come to know the truth).

In Frank Capra's classic movie, "It's a Wonderful Life," Clarence the angel tells George: "Strange isn't it? Each man's life touches so many other lives. When he isn't around, he leaves an awful hole, doesn't he?" "Remember George: "No man is a failure who has friends."

One cannot help but notice one of the phrases used in the Bible is "one another." We are to love one another. George Bailey's father told him, "All you can take with you is that which you've given away." Jesus says when we did it to one of the least of these my brothers, you did it unto me." Matthew 25.

What a friend we have in Jesus, all our griefs and sins to bear. He is watching for you. I was captivated recently when my son John sent a short video of our granddaughter, Sloan, running in the park. She runs with such joy. When the Lord sees you a great way off, headed for home, just call His name, and He will come running with great joy!

"You've Got A Friend"[29]

Carole King was one of the most prolific and successful female song writers and, later, performers for the latter part of the 20th century. Her records have sold an estimated 75 million copies.

She possessed perfect pitch. Her list of songs go back to early rock and roll like "Loco-Motion" by Little Eva, to "Go Away Little Girl" by Steve Lawrence. Aretha Franklin's signature, "Natural Woman," and so many others, including "You've Got a Friend."

Ms. King said this song practically wrote itself. Ironically, she said she was inspired by a line in James Taylor's "Fire and Rain": that "I've seen lonely times when I could not find a friend." Think about loneliness of that magnitude—where you cannot find a friend.

We all want to have friends. Someone we can depend on to be there when we need them. From television shows like, "Friends" to "Cheers" everyone wants to go somewhere where everybody knows their name.

It is a universal need which goes back to the fact when Adam was alone on planet earth, God said, "It is not good for man to be alone."

---

[29] Written by Carole King. Recorded by: Carole King, also James Taylor. Released: January 1971. Charts: Taylor's version went to No.1. King's Album, "Tapestry" went to NO.1 in 1971 and stayed on the charts for the next 6 years.

You've got a friend who will stick closer than a brother. You've got a friend in Jesus.

A WORD FROM THE AUTHORS

If you are a believer, we hope this will encourage you to share your faith with those whom God brings into your life who do not know the true and living God. We believe God is who He says He is and can do what He says He can do. Creation is a good place to start. Where did all this come from? Why is there something rather than nothing? Asking questions is how we learn. There are four questions we want to set before you. Your answer to these four questions will form your worldview. We believe each person must consider their answers to these four questions thoughtfully and seriously for they determine how we live our lives.

1. Origin: From where or what source did all of this universe come? The Bible says the heavens declare the glory of God, as does a butterfly, hummingbirds, flowers, mountains, sunsets, snow, rainbows, giraffes and babies. Who or what caused all of this? Your answer will form your worldview and should tell you from whence you came.

2. Purpose: What is the purpose and meaning of life? Is 'life a tale told by an idiot full of sound and fury, signifying nothing', as Shakespeare wrote? Or is it as Longfellow wrote: "Tell me not in mournful numbers, life is but an empty dream. And the soul is dead that slumbers and things are not as they seem. Life is real! Life is earnest! And the grave is not the goal.

Dust thou art to dust returneth was not spoken of the soul."

3. Morals: How does one determine right from wrong? Good or evil? Is there a fixed point of reference? Or is there simply a sliding scale which adapts to social whims? If there is not a fixed point of reference for morals, no standards, then one will do what "feels right." The Bible says, "There is a way which seems right to man, but it leads to destruction."

4. Destiny: Is there life after death? Probably debated by most everyone and addressed by many different faiths, beliefs and ideas. Does your world view have the explanatory power to answer these questions to your satisfaction? Have you considered the source on which you have formed your opinion?

Remember, everyone has to believe something extraordinary to answer these questions. Science in the 20th century revealed the universe had not always existed. The universe began with a "big bang." If there is a "big bang," there must be a Big Banger.

If you are one who doubts the Bible is nothing more than an ancient book written by men, are you an honest doubter or a dishonest doubter? An honest doubter wants to know the truth, an explanation which makes sense. A dishonest doubter comes with a bias and looks for reasons not to believe, rather than believe.

Gina and I want to encourage you to read the Gospels. These are four books about the life and ministry of Jesus. It might just give you an *idea* about who this Jesus really is. Remember *ideas have consequences.*

Tim and Gina Fortner

ABOUT THE AUTHORS

Tim and Gina Fortner

Tim and Gina grew up 28 miles apart from each other in West Tennessee. They grew up in the same era of music, movies and events. They went off to different colleges in the '60s. Tim started out as a history major and Gina as a music major. She would later become a registered nurse and Tim a salesman in the optical industry. They met in 1975 while Gina was a nursing student. Their courtship, falling in love and getting married was against a backdrop of music to which they danced and danced and still dance.

Their marriage would result in three children, Carrie, John and Ben. Tim would have a successful career in the optical industry and end up traveling around the world speaking and training on behalf of a new company called Transitions Optical. Gina would work as a nurse, but her main role was mother to three children who were born in a four-year period. Life was busy and passed in a blur of school trips, athletic events, piano recitals and family vacations to the beach. Three children in braces, three teenage drivers, and three children in college kept our "noses to the grindstone." But they were special years.

Tim started teaching an adult Bible class in 1989 and continues to do so to this day. It would become his most important work. Gina was and is a prayer warrior. She taught her children and now her grandchildren about the Lord. Memorization of Scripture has given her a powerful testimony as she has gone through the fiery trials of cancer not once, but twice. Tim battled alcohol in his college and early adult days and has been in recovery for over 40 years.

They have come to believe this is the time for us Baby Boomers to stand up for the Word of God. We inherited a country for which our parents and grandparents worked so hard to give us. Now it is time for us to pass on to the next generation the faith and principles which made our parents' generation the greatest generation of the 20th century. When we look at the state of our union today, we realize we have some of our most important work before us. We need to pass on our faith and stories to the next generation. We urge you to write your story and testimony to give to your family. It will be something they cherish in the years to come. Who knows? For such a time as this you came into the kingdom of God.

PEOPLE GET READY

For speaking events contact Tim at: **johntfortner@gmail.com**. You can also visit the website for Tim's lesson notes at:

www.timfortner.com

EPILOGUE

PEOPLE GET READY. How does one prepare when leaving on a vacation? They make reservations. The Gospel is an invitation to accept the finished work of the Lord Jesus Christ. But one must respond to the invitation.

At the beginning of this book, we extended an invitation Jesus Himself extends to you. He has invited you to "come and see." More than once, we referred to how He knocks on the door of your heart awaiting an invitation to come into your life.

Let us present the simple elements of the Gospel. They are threefold:

1. *Jesus died for our sins, according to the Scriptures. This is of first importance*
2. *Jesus was buried. This is proof of His death.*
3. *Jesus rose on the third day according to Scriptures. He was subsequently seen by over 500 witnesses. (I Corinthians 15: 1-11)*

Jesus died for our sins, mine and yours and the sins of the whole world. He was the substitute for our sins. He paid in full the price for our sins. He paid with His life . His blood cleanses us from all our sins. His resurrection in a glorified body is proof of God's acceptance of His Sacrifice.

It's about a simple message,
And whether you believe.
It's still the cross,
It's still the blood of Calvary;
That cleanses sin,

And sets the captive free,
It's still the name of Jesus,
That has the power to save the lost.
It's still the cross.
(It's Still the Cross, by Luke Garrett.)

The Invitation

Would you like to receive the Lord Jesus as your Savior? To do so, we invite you to pray this prayer:

Dear God:

I know I am a sinner. I ask you for your forgiveness of all my sins. I believe the Good News that Christ died for my sins and You raised Him from the dead. I want to trust Him as my Savior and follow Jesus as my Lord from this day forward. Come into my life Lord Jesus and guide me in Your will. I pray this in the name of Jesus. Amen.

RSVP are the initials which stand for: *Responde Sil Vous Plait (French) meaning: respond if you please.*

An invitation can be responded to in three ways:

1. *You can ignore the invitation and your non-response is counted as a NO.*
2. *You can respond NO, not accepting the invitation.*
3. *You can answer YES and you will be saved from your sins.*

"If you confess with your mouth the Lord Jesus and believe in your heart God has raised Him from the dead, you will be saved. For with the heart one believes unto righteousness, and with the mouth confession is made unto salvation. For the Scripture

says, *"Whoever believes on Him will not be put shame. For whoever calls on the name of the Lord shall be saved." Romans 10.*

Gina and I have prayed you will say YES to this invitation. God wants you say, "Yes," more than anything.

It really is about a simple message and whether you believe. It's still the Cross of Calvary.

Please let us know if you have prayed this prayer.

-Tim and Gina Fortner
johntfortner@gmail.com

Made in the USA
Columbia, SC
19 September 2020